THE
NATIONAL
REVIEW
OBAMA
READER

Selected Essays and Articles on
The One We Have Been Waiting For
2007-2010

Richard Lowry, Mark Steyn, Jonah Goldberg,
Andrew C. McCarthy, Victor Davis Hanson,
John O'Sullivan, Stanley Kurtz, Ramesh Ponnuru,
Andrew Stuttaford, Stephen Spruiell, Fred Siegel,
Rob Long, Mark Hemingway, Allen C. Guelzo,
Byron York, John J. Miller, Jamie M. Fly,
Michael Gledhill, Michael Knox Beran

To obtain additional or bulk copies of
this collection please contact:

National Review
Re: The Obama Reader
215 Lexington Avenue, 11th Floor
New York, NY 10016

ISBN 0-9758998-5-6

Please visit our website at
www.nationalreview.com

National Review thanks Kathryn Murdock, Christeleny
Frangos, Amy Tyler, Sara Towne, Aleks Karnick, and
Luba Myts for the many duties they performed to help
bring this book to fruition.

PRINTED IN THE UNITED STATES OF AMERICA

TABLE OF CONTENTS

SECTION ONE: BLACK OBAMA

SECTION TWO: FAKE OBAMA

SECTION THREE: SIDEKICK OBAMA

SECTION FOUR: POST-AMERICAN OBAMA

SECTION FIVE: REAL OBAMA

BLACK
OBAMA

June 2, 2008

Beneath the Hope

Obama and the politics of grievance

By Victor Davis Hanson

The more Barack Obama racks up majorities in states with large university and black populations—what Clinton strategist Paul Begala called the "eggheads and African-Americans"—the more he seems to fare poorly in the electoral-vote-rich states that will be in play in November, most of which have large white working-class constituencies. Indeed, he may be the first Democratic nominee in memory to lose the primary elections in California, Indiana, New Jersey, New York, Ohio, Pennsylvania, and Texas.

Barack Obama talks passionately about hope, change—and racial transcendence. But what advanced him this far was not merely his eloquence, but also his ability simultaneously to play on, and disguise, the politics of racial grievance. And yet he seems confused and angry when reminded that such a doctrine won't quite deliver him the presidency. When the anti-American remarks of Rev. Jeremiah Wright were widely aired, Obama seemed at first taken aback. Why would anyone be outraged? After all, there was nothing secret about Wright. Obama had even quoted, in his memoir, Wright's accusations that white America was responsible for everything from world hunger to genocide against the Japanese, and had bragged in speeches about his intimacy with Wright.

So Obama was naturally confused by the outcry. At first he thought he could shrug his way out of it with the quip that the Trinity congregation was not "particularly controversial"; Wright himself, in Obama's words, was "brilliant" and a "respected Biblical scholar." Yet within days Obama resorted to a different defense: Wright was not much more out of the mainstream than the proverbial outspoken and often embarrassing "old uncle." After that, Obama ended up offering several additional explanations, among them an inspirational speech on race—which unexpectedly turned out to be a sort of get-out-of-jail-free card for Wright, who later at the National Press Club confirmed that his earlier inane rants about whites, the AIDS virus, and American culpability for 9/11 in fact were not taken out of context but deeply embedded in his worldview.

For all Obama's eloquence, his clean-up campaign contextualized the serial Wright venom within the familiar saga of grievance and racial victimization: Whites do not understand the theatrical protocols of Wright's black church. The prior good works of Wright in community outreach and anti-apartheid activism outweigh his occasional unfortunate speech. Wright's slurs were taken out of context. Wright had been turned into a convenient tool for right-wing politicos. In short, Obama was reduced to pleading on March 18, "I can no more disown him [Wright] than I can my white grandmother—a woman who helped raise me."

But, of course, that blanket amnesty for Wright became inoperative after the enterprising Wright's National Press Club rant of April 28, whose insulting tone elicited outrage among the liberal Washington press corps, and thus required yet another Obama protestation: "It is antithetical to our campaign. It is antithetical to what I'm about. It is not what I think America stands for. Reverend Wright does not speak for me. He does not speak for our campaign. I cannot prevent him from making these outrageous remarks. . . . When I say that I find these statements appalling, I mean it . . . makes me angry but also saddens me."

Wright, of course, said nothing on April 28 that he had not said previously. To his credit, Wright has been consistent in his views, odious though they may be. It is Obama who on five or six occasions has changed his story about Wright—always under pressure, and always in reaction to the public's, rather than his own, outrage at Wright.

IT'S NOT JUST WRIGHT

Meanwhile, Michelle Obama, the candidate's wife, was reported airing her own grievances about a "just downright mean" America. Her serial complaints culminated in the now infamous "For the first time in my adult life, I am proud of my country." That revelation, voiced on two separate occasions, raised a storm of protest, since it seemed to confirm that Wright's anti-American message had been absorbed into the Obama worldview after the couple's 20 years of attendance at his church.

The most controversial of the growing list of Obama grievances and clumsy retractions was Barack's dismissal of Pennsylvania's small-town, middle-America culture: "And it's not surprising then they get bitter, they cling to guns or religion or antipathy to people who aren't like them or anti-immigrant sentiment or anti-trade sentiment as a way to explain their frustrations."

Like Reverend Wright's mendacious views on 9/11 and AIDS, almost everything in that sentence was either untrue or disingenuous. Pennsylvanians valued gun ownership and religion for centuries before the supposed current economic downturn—and while times are perceived as rough, the unemployment rate in Pennsylvania is still about 5 percent. Obama himself has whipped up "anti-trade sentiment" by trashing NAFTA and similar proposed trade accords.

That he gave this speech in liberal, upscale San Francisco only added to the aura of condescension—especially the standard liberal trope of false consciousness: The ignorant working classes turn toward extraneous palliatives rather than follow the advice of Harvard intellectuals to agitate for economic redistribution that would better solve their mostly material problems. Had Hillary Clinton used the same sort of "they" language—say in front of a conservative, midwestern white audience—to explain why inner-city, gun-toting, church-attending blacks were turning out en masse for Obama, her campaign would have been rightly finished then and there.

Michelle resonated these same themes of liberal superciliousness when she announced that "Barack is one of the smartest people you will ever encounter who will deign to enter this messy thing called politics." She even expanded on Barack's dismissal of Pennsylvanians, by suggesting that all of America suffers from the same blinkered parochialism: "Barack will never allow you to go back to your lives as usual, uninvolved, uninformed."

More disturbing than the original grievance was Obama's rationalization for his Pennsylvania comment. He didn't apologize for the sentiments expressed, but instead lamely pleaded that he might have "mangled" or "conflated" what he intended to say. Later Obama suggested that his message about Middle America's misery and bitterness was true. But when Obama's formal clarification of Pennsylvania's problems followed, it once again only emphasized his accustomed slipperiness: "So people they vote about guns, or they take comfort from their faith and their family and their community. And they get mad about illegal immigrants who are coming over to this country or they get frustrated about, you know, how things are changing. That's a natural response."

Note how the original "cling" now becomes "vote about" and "take comfort from." Likewise, "antipathy to people who aren't like them" morphs into "their family and their community"—as fundamentalist xenophobes are really just beleaguered folks who band together. Obama lectured the San Francisco–area wealthy about the "anti-immigrant" scapegoating habits of Middle Americans. But he really meant, or so he later said, that they are merely "mad about illegal immigrants." Note again, in the clarification, how Obama's nativists, who oppose all immigrants, legal and illegal, transform into reasonable people becoming understandably angry only about those coming here illegally.

Yet when all that still didn't work, Obama simply said he was a churchgoer himself, so how could he ridicule devout Pennsylvanians?—omitting altogether that he had slurred them as clinging to "antipathy to people who aren't like them or anti-immigrant sentiment."

SILVER SPOONS
Why do the affluent, astute Obamas cling to such doctrinaire grievances, and then offer insulting clarifications when called on them? The obvious explanation is that Barack Obama had previously navigated only on the small lakes of the Ivy League and Chicago politics, where the drumbeat of grievance pays real dividends and easy anti-American throw-off lines are hardly gaffes. But now, for the first time in his life, he is buffeted by the gales of an ever-widening national campaign where his once-persuasive themes suddenly sound absurd.

The problem with Obama's former habitat—and the Democratic-primary landscape—is not just that activist blacks, students, and Ivy Leaguers are not a good cross-section of the American population.

Rather, such sympathetic audiences ensured that every whine that he and his wife have voiced over 20 years has been applauded rather than examined—and so they became deeply ingrained in the Obama psyche. When pressed on Wright's Press Club slurs, Michelle Obama announced: "You know what I think. . . . We've got to move forward. You know, this conversation doesn't help my kids." With Michelle, it is never about reassuring "uninvolved, uniformed" Americans that she condemns Wright, the abject racist—but always about her own family's travails.

An upscale Chicago neighborhood hardly thinks that past familiarity with self-described bomber Bill Ayers is a liability. If an Obama associate like Rev. James Meeks blasts homosexuals, or Los Angeles Obama supporter Rev. Eric Lee spouts anti-Semitic drivel, they do so under the accepted cover that black victims cannot themselves be victimizers. And Reverend Wright's tirades no more offended 8,000 in the present congregation of Trinity Church than they apparently did the Obamas, who, far from walking out, simply refined Wright in softer and more elegant terms in their own writings and speeches. Those at Columbia or Harvard readily buy into the *What's the Matter with Kansas?* pop neo-Marxism—namely, that the Democratic party's inability to garner a majority of the electorate is caused entirely by the fact that Karl Rove's Republicans confuse and manipulate ignorant yokels, who, in their desperation and fear, stupidly retreat to guns, God, and racism.

So in his defense, Obama was only voicing what is now the elitist doctrine of many Democrats. *Newsweek* essayist Michael Hirsh recently scoffed that the problem with the white working class that mysteriously cannot appreciate Obama goes back to the pathological nature of American history that plagues us still: "The outcome was that a substantial portion of the new nation developed, over many generations, a rather savage, unsophisticated set of mores. Traditionally, it has been balanced by a more diplomatic, communitarian Yankee sensibility from the Northeast and upper Midwest. But that latter sensibility has been losing ground in population numbers—and cultural weight."

Given his worldview, it's entirely predictable that Obama will continue, if inadvertently, to voice grievances that offend those in Middle America. He can win the Democratic nomination the same way McGovern, Mondale, Dukakis, and Kerry did—by appealing to an activist-liberal base. And he will never really offer unequivocal apologies for what he declares or what his associates say, because he doesn't feel he's done anything wrong—at least by the standards of his past that are continually buttressed by his campaign staff and much of the mainstream media. Better for all of them to blame Pennsylvania, the white working class, or the illiberal southern and frontier strains within American history for the fact that Obama's genius is insufficiently appreciated.

Obama thinks mea culpas are not necessary, because his eloquence will always remedy what offends. That's why someone who was named by *National Journal* as the Senate's most doctrinaire liberal can, with a straight face, persuade millions that he is running on a record of bipartisanship. Obama may advocate engaging Iran's President Ahmadinejad, who has advocated the annihilation of Israel; but he can also condemn Jimmy Carter's recent embrace of Hamas leaders with, "We must not negotiate with a terrorist group intent on Israel's destruction."

Obama frequently resorts to false analogy. For him, as we have seen, context is everything—and it is often established by false comparison. So, for example, Reverend Wright is not *that* venomous, but a sort of everyman's eccentric uncle—as if we could choose blood relatives as we do pastors. Wright's racism is shared by all, and not meant to be pernicious, in the manner that his grandmother's fear of young black males on the street is that of a "typical white person"—as if one were right to embarrass a once-nurturing but now-aged grandmother to absolve a political crony; as if there were not statistics suggesting that black male youths are more prone to commit violent crimes than their white and Asian counterparts.

According to Obama, unrepentant bomber Bill Ayers is analogous to Tom Coburn, a Republican senator from Oklahoma and a physician, who once suggested that laws might be drafted allowing capital punishment for the abortionist—as if the terrorist were morally equivalent to the physician-senator. This is 1960s relativism and "they do it too" at its very worst.

It's not just inexperience or the climate of the Democratic party, but also the current state of race relations that ensures the Obamas will continue to say things they should not—and then make it worse by rationalizing what they say. For all the incessant calls for a "national conversation about race," racial grievance is about all we have been talking about the past few years. But it has been an unfortunate one-way sermon, in which well-off black activists lament the legacy of slavery, present-day racism, and the need for various forms of reparations, while their white interlocutors accept that there is to be no reference to miseries within the black community that are not explicable by mere prejudice—such as inordinate rates of drug use, illegitimacy, and crime.

True "conversations" cannot proceed, because all sorts of taboo topics cannot be raised—from the success of Asians and other minorities to the previous successful integration of millions of blacks into the mainstream of American life. We saw that one-sided dialogue on the airwaves, with too many black intellectuals defending Wright by redefining Martin Luther King down as a similar principled firebrand, by arguing that there was often truth to Wright's slanders, and by associating him with widely shared and legitimate black angst—until Wright embarrassed them all by deliberately going after Obama and insulting a sympathetic white-liberal D.C. press corps.

A Reverend Wright cannot move into a multimillion-dollar estate of over 10,000 square feet by downplaying racial differences, much less by preaching racial reconciliation and self-help. He lacks the talent and character of a Clarence Thomas, Condoleezza Rice, or Colin Powell—indeed, he lacks the ability of the millions in the black middle class that he serially damns. Instead Wright profits by lambasting black "middle-classness," the U.S., and white people. This offers a sort of Sunday venting for some blacks who in effect hire him to "contextualize" and transfer their personal failures and complaints onto some higher plane of cosmic racism—which may well bring them government or social compensation, both material and psychological.

The culmination of Wright's audacity, and his complete confidence in the exemption that his apparent black authenticity provides, was his infamous April 27 keynote address to the Detroit NAACP's 53rd Annual Fight for Freedom Fund dinner, in which he delineated racial differences between blacks and "Europeans" in their respective manners of learning. Wright outlined a "right brain" black emphasis on spirituality and musicality versus a white "left brain" aptitude for analysis and logic; it was just the sort of Bell Curve racialism that at one time earned blanket con-demnation. But it won Wright a standing ovation from an audience of the nation's premier civil-rights organization (and brought not a word of condemnation from Obama himself).

SOURCES OF OBAMA CONDUCT

Obama learned from, but radically refined, this racial approach. A Barry Obama who never attended Trinity Church—one who would write not a memoir called *Dreams from My Father*, but a more accurate one called *Dreams from My Grandparents*, in praise of those who raised him—would be evaluated entirely on his own merits. He would find it difficult to transmogrify into a racial sensation who appeals to, and is used by, a host of others. In political terms, that might have made him a charismat-ic and eloquent black congressman of mixed heritage, one who ignores race—like the talented and successful former congressman Harold Ford Jr. If Obama had been a white media sensation, a newcomer without con-gressional accomplishment, he might have matched the third-place finish of suave John Edwards. Without either racial packaging or legislative accomplishment, a talented first-term senator surely would not become a president—as liberals from Black Entertainment Television billionaire Robert Johnson to veteran politico Geraldine Ferraro have pointed out.

Instead, *Harvard Law Review* editor Barack Obama had to sit through years of Wright's lunacy *precisely* to prove to his future local constituents that he would air their grievances, and to establish his own bona fides as a voice of the ghetto oppressed. Once these street creden-tials were painfully acquired, the Ivy League-educated Obama would—like Wright—win a guilt-free context for an elite lifestyle, and a politi-cal base from which to transcend, soaring with a message of social and racial misery. It is a winning combination: Unlike black conservatives, Obama taps into the identity politics of victimization and grievance; unlike white liberals, he resonates racial authenticity; and, unlike race hustlers such as Al Sharpton or Reverend Wright, he is consistently elo-quent rather than at times crude and off-putting.

The Obamas may have made over $4 million in 2007, but Michelle can still credibly preach on the stump that a nebulous "they" raised the bar on them—as Ivy League loans, private school, camp for the kids, and costly piano lessons do their part to take them down. The "man" of the 'hood—the "man" who smothers black aspirations—is ubiquitous. Indeed, Michelle can testify that he becomes "they" who hound blacks even in the white suburbs after they have become millionaires: "Folks set the bar, and then you work hard and you reach the bar—sometimes you surpass the bar—and then *they* move the bar!"

To the Obamas, the multifarious "they" are also sometimes the illiberal white working classes, who did not accept hope and change and lost Obama Pennsylvania and now Indiana. For Michelle, another "they" changed the rules of campaigning and made the Obamas raise ever more cash and become ever more organized: "*They* tell you to raise money, you raise money. *They* tell you to build an organization, and you build an organization."

If, to acquire lucre and power, a Jeremiah Wright realized that he had to allow angrier blacks from time to time to vent their unhappiness by articulating the role of sinister cosmic forces—such as government-induced HIV viruses and magic bombs that target only blacks and Arabs—a Barack Obama sensed that he could trump that, by franchising his politics of grievance to a new neighborhood of affluent white intellectuals and professionals. Obama gave his Pennsylvania "they cling" speech to a nodding Bay Area audience. While white elites lack the economic resentments of Reverend Wright's flock, they have psychological needs that a mellifluous Obama brilliantly discovered how to address.

Their zealotry for Obama singularly reassures white liberal elites that they really are empathetic to minority needs, but need not feel that their own riches came at the expense of others. Through her *Huffington Post*, Arianna Huffington can voice the Obama concern for the oppressed while cruising the shores of Tahiti in David Geffen's 452-foot yacht. So there is no reason to join a Trinity outreach program to tutor the ghetto youngster, or dismantle the wall around the gated compound, when you can put an Obama sign on your Brentwood lawn. Abroad, the dividends are even greater. A President Barack Hussein Obama, who emblemizes grievance and contrition, can refashion America's global image. The affluent liberal American wants to be liked every bit as much as he wants to enjoy his hybrid Mercedes, his granite countertops, and having a daughter at Princeton.

This is the maze that Obama worked through in brilliant fashion—in Chicago, in Illinois statewide, and in the primaries. But now, as the general election looms, he is in a much larger, more unfamiliar labyrinth, and he hasn't quite figured it out yet—even though a war, a troubled economy, and an unpopular Republican president have given him openings not available to other Democrats since the post-Watergate election of 1976.

Most Americans are tired of racial victimization and opportunism, especially as the country becomes more multiracial, with a myriad of competing grievances. They haven't elected a northern liberal president since JFK, nearly half a century ago. They don't like hypocritical elites preaching to them about their supposedly reactionary habits. And yet some of their votes are still essential, if one wishes to win the presidency.

So the question remains how quickly an adept, adaptable, and seemingly unprincipled Barack Obama will come to understand that he can no longer say—or contextualize—what was so successful in bringing him this far. Instead, in Bill Clinton fashion, from time to time he will have to bite his lip, look humbled—and then simply apologize for the silly grievances he voices and the even sillier people that for so long he has befriended. If he cannot do that, then the next six months will be characterized by more smug, off-the-cuff dismissals of middling America, more innate condescension from Michelle Obama, still more racism from the malicious Reverend Wright, more skeletons yet to appear out of Barack Obama's vast progressive cemetery of the last 20 years—and, by October, the greatest case of Democratic buyer's remorse since the McGovern campaign of midsummer 1972.

June 30, 2008

True Believer

Obama was for black-liberation theology before he was against it

By Stanley Kurtz

By this point, nobody can seriously suggest that Barack Obama was unaware of the hate-filled rhetoric emanating from the pulpit at Trinity United Church of Christ until it was, very recently, pointed out to him. The church's long history of radical-leftist and anti-white sermons by Jeremiah Wright, Michael Pfleger, and others has been made so unmistakably clear that even the mainstream media eventually had to notice, forcing the candidate to offer his half-hearted resignation from the church. With that act, Obama hoped to close the book on his Trinity connection, putting an end to the questions about what he knew and when, and why he waited so long to leave the church.

A more interesting question, though, is why Obama joined Trinity in the first place. Some of his defenders suggest he did so to advance his career as a community organizer: The residents he needed to reach and the contacts he needed to make went to Trinity, so he went there too. In this view, Obama was merely being practical, not radical.

Don't believe it. This was no matter of convenience or expediency. Obama's connections to the radical-left politics espoused by Pfleger and Wright are broad and deep, and he largely approved of their political-theological outlook. Obama shared Wright's rejection of black "assimilation," individual self-improvement, and the pursuit of "middle-classness." His goal was not to repudiate religious radicalism but to channel its fervor into an effective and permanent activist organization. How do we know all this? We know it because Obama himself has told us.

A key source for deciphering his political views is a 1995 background piece on Obama that appeared in the *Chicago Reader*, a left-leaning "alternative" weekly. Hank De Zutter's "What Makes Obama Run?" gives us an in-depth picture of Obama's worldview on the eve of his career in electoral politics. In it, Obama presents his political hopes for the black community as a third way between two inadequate alternatives.

First he rejects, in De Zutter's words, "the unrealistic politics of integrationist assimilation—which helps a few upwardly mobile blacks to 'move up, get rich, and move out.' " Obama, we are told, "quickly learned that integration was a one-way street, with blacks expected to assimilate into a white world that never gave ground." He also criticizes "the politics of black rage and black nationalism"—although less on substance than on tactics. De Zutter says Obama is "tired of seeing the moral fervor of black folks whipped up—at the speaker's rostrum and from the pulpit—and then allowed to dissipate because there's no agenda, no concrete program for change." The problem is not the fiery rhetoric, but merely the wasted anger.

De Zutter lays out Obama's ties to such radical groups as Chicago ACORN, whose lead organizer at the time, Madeline Talbott, practiced the sort of intimidating and often illegal "direct action" that ACORN remains famous for. Talbott is quoted affirming that "Barack has proven himself among our members . . . we accept and respect him as a kindred spirit, a fellow organizer." The article also mentions Obama's early organizing work for the Developing Communities Project, which was "funded by south-side Catholic churches." Clearly, this early work cemented Obama's close ties to Father Pfleger, whose support formed a critical component of Obama's grassroots network. Because of this early link, Pfleger threw his considerable support behind Obama's failed 2000 bid for Congress.

In an article on National Review Online, I explored the possibility that Obama may also have used his seats on the boards of a couple of liberal Chicago foundations to direct funds to groups that served as his de facto political base. The threads of this political network are pulled tighter as Obama turns to a "favorite topic": "the lack of collective action among black churches." In this year's presidential campaign, Obama has rationalized his ties to Trinity Church by citing its community-service programs. Yet in 1995 he was highly critical of churches that focused exclusively on food pantries and other services while neglecting the sort of politically visionary sermons, local king-making, and political alliance-building favored by Pfleger and Wright.

Obama rejected the strictly community-service approach of apolitical churches as part of America's unfortunate "bias" toward "individual action." He derogated this as "John Wayne" thinking and the old "right wing . . . individualistic bootstrap myth," which needs to be replaced: "We have some wonderful preachers in town—preachers who continue to inspire me—preachers who are magnificent at articulating a vision of the world as it should be. . . . But as soon as church lets out, the energy dissipates. We must find ways to channel all this energy into community building." If anything, Obama wanted to give the political visions of Wright and Pfleger greater weight and substance, by connecting them to secular-leftist political networks like ACORN.

Another part of Obama's strategy was to stay outside traditional political channels. As a Chicago organizer and attorney, Obama took care to maintain friendly ties to the Daley administration, but in his 1996 campaign for state senate, he specifically avoided asking the mayor or the mayor's closest allies for support. Obama's plan was to make an end run around Chicago's governing Democratic political network by building a coalition of left-leaning black churches and radical secular organizations like ACORN (perhaps with de facto help from liberal-foundation money as well). This coalition would provide Obama with the flexibility to play out a political career some distance to the left of conventional Illinois Democratic politics. And sure enough, Obama's extremely liberal record in Illinois proved to be of a piece with his strategy.

It could be argued that the new and supposedly moderate Obama of 2008 is the real Obama. Unfortunately, that argument is unconvincing. As De Zutter notes, Obama gave up a near-certain Supreme Court clerkship to come to Chicago and do community organizing, so he must have felt strongly about it. (See "The Organizer," by Byron York, on page 127.) He could have joined one of the many other, less-radical black churches on the South Side of Chicago, if that was all he needed to launch a political career. And given his good relations with the Daley administration, Obama could have asked for its support in his bid for the state senate. Yet at every turn, Obama took a riskier path. That suggests he was operating from conviction. Trouble is, the conviction in question was apparently Obama's belief in the sort of radical social and economic views held by groups like ACORN and preachers like Wright and Pfleger.

If there is any doubt about the accuracy of De Zutter's detailed account, we get the same message from a little-discussed but revealing and important piece by Obama himself. In 1988, just after he joined Trinity, Obama wrote an article titled "Why Organize? Problems and Promise in the Inner City" (which was reprinted in the 1990 book *After Alinsky: Community Organizing in Illinois*). It shows exactly what Obama hoped to make of his association with Pfleger and Wright.

Obama begins by rejecting the false dichotomy between radicalism and moderation: "From W. E. B. DuBois to Booker T. Washington to Marcus Garvey to Malcolm X to Martin Luther King, this internal debate has raged between integration and nationalism, between accommodation and militancy, between sit-down strikes and boardroom negotiations." Unsurprisingly, Obama proposes to use the best from both approaches. Of course, even James Cone, the radical founder of black-liberation theology, sees himself as synthesizing the moderation of Martin Luther King Jr. with the radicalism of Malcolm X.

Obama continues: "Nowhere is the promise of organizing more apparent than in the traditional black churches. Possessing tremendous financial resources, membership and—most importantly—values and biblical traditions that call for empowerment and liberation, the black church is clearly a slumbering giant in the political and economic landscape of cities like Chicago." After expressing disappointment with apolitical black churches focused only on traditional community services, Obama goes on to point in a more activist direction:

> Over the past few years, however, more and more young and forward-thinking pastors have begun to look at community organizations such as the Developing Communities Project in the far south side . . . as a powerful tool for living the social gospel, one which can educate and empower entire congregations and not just serve as a platform for a few prophetic leaders. Should a mere 50 prominent black church-

es, out of thousands that exist in cities like Chicago, decide to collaborate with a trained and organized staff, enormous positive changes could be wrought.

Give me 50 Pflegers or 50 Wrights, Obama is saying, tie them to a network of grassroots activists like my companions from ACORN, and we can revolutionize urban politics.

So it would appear that Obama's own writings solve the mystery of why he stayed at Trinity for 20 years. Obama's long-held and decidedly audacious hope has been to spread Wright's radical spirit by linking it to a viable, left-leaning political program, with Obama himself at the center. The revolutionizing power of a politically awakened black church is not a side issue, or merely a personal matter, but has been the signature theme of Obama's grand political strategy.

After the 2004 election, there was some talk of the Democratic party's "purging" such radical elements as MoveOn and Michael Moore. Far from purging its radical Left, however, the Democratic party is now just inches away from placing it in the driver's seat. That is the real meaning of the fiasco at Trinity Church.

September 1, 2008

Quota Quest

Of Obama's vulnerability on racial preferences

By John J. Miller

The election of Barack Obama threatens to become the worst thing that ever happened to race-based affirmative action. So says liberal columnist Bonnie Erbe. "What could do more damage to the argument that African Americans deserve racial preferences than a majority of Americans voting to put an African American in the White House?" she asked in July. Her answer: "Little, from where I sit."

The case for racial preferences almost certainly would weaken during an Obama presidency. Sanctimonious liberals everywhere would face a squirm-inducing question: "If racism in America is so bad, then how come . . . ?" The smart ones will observe that most whites actually cast their votes for John McCain (as seems likely, based on current polls). Even so, Obama's success would force the conversation about racial preferences to shift fundamentally.

To a certain extent, it already has. On the night of January 26, after Obama won South Carolina's Democratic primary, supporters at a victory party broke into a chant: "Race doesn't matter! Race doesn't matter!" The mood was so jubilant that even a veteran race hustler like Rev. Jeremiah Wright would have been tempted to join in.

Yet the case for racial preferences and their ongoing reality are separate things. Obama may inspire all kinds of happy talk about national healing. (If you think the media are already treating him as a post-racial messiah, just wait until his inauguration day.) At the same time, his administration would strive to make sure that racial bean-counting shaped voting districts, college admissions, K–12 demographics, public contracting, and business hiring.

Personnel is policy, and Obama almost certainly would nominate judges and appoint civil-rights officials from the ranks of activist organizations whose very purpose is to push the idea that race matters, contrary to what those South Carolina chanters had the audacity to hope. Just translate the name of a leading Hispanic group, the National Council of La Raza: In complete English, it's the National Council of *the Race.*

Obama isn't special in this regard. Nearly any Democrat in the White House would draw from the same pool of people and advance the same color-coded causes. Raul Yzaguirre, who served as president of the National Council of the Race for three decades, was a co-chairman of Hillary Clinton's presidential campaign.

Some foes of racial preferences nevertheless have felt the urge to cheer on Obama, in the belief that his success represents at least a symbolic victory for colorblindness. Ward Connerly is both a Republican and America's best-known foe of racial preferences. In February, he sent a $500 donation to Obama. "My token contribution wasn't an endorsement," says Connerly, who supported Rudy Giuliani in the GOP primaries and now plans to vote for McCain. "But I wanted to applaud his efforts to take America beyond race."

Although Obama's campaign cashed Connerly's check, the Democrat has refused to pay back any respects. In fact, he's done quite the opposite. On July 27, McCain endorsed the Arizona Civil Rights Initiative—a Connerly-led ballot referendum that would ban racial preferences in the state. Later that day, Obama pounced, in remarks at a conference of minority journalists: "I think in the past [McCain had] been opposed to these Ward Connerly initiatives as divisive. And I think he's right. These are not designed to solve a big problem, but they're all too often designed to drive a wedge between people."

The first point was fair enough: In the past, McCain has blasted efforts to ban racial preferences. He once even labeled them "divisive." McCain doesn't like to admit changing his mind, but apparently he has—in a direction that's both more conservative and more in keeping with public sentiment. Connerly's initiatives, after all, have passed in the Democrat-leaning states of California, Michigan, and Washington. In November, they're likely to appear on ballots in Arizona, Colorado, and

Nebraska. No wonder Obama sees them as divisive: They set him apart from the views of most Americans, at a time when he's trying to become broadly acceptable.

Obama has a long history of backing racial preferences. As a state senator in Illinois, he called them "absolutely necessary." Nothing changed when he moved to Washington. The man who recently spoke in Berlin about the need to tear down "the walls between races and tribes" has supported a bill that would recognize ethnic Hawaiians as a federal tribe with a series of race-based privileges. Two years ago, Obama recorded a radio ad in which he urged Michigan voters to rally against Proposal 2, the Connerly initiative: "It would wipe out programs that help women and minorities get a good education and jobs. . . . It moves us further away from a country of full opportunity."

As a presidential candidate, Obama has tried to sound more conciliatory. When the topic of racial preferences comes up, he says he's against quotas—politicians always say they're against quotas—and suggests considering class-based preferences. "We have to think about affirmative action and craft it in such a way where some of our children who are advantaged aren't getting more favorable treatment than a poor white kid who has struggled more," he said in July. But make no mistake: Obama would not supplant racial preferences with socioeconomic ones. Instead, he might supplement them, further chipping away at the notion that merit ought to outweigh all else when awarding anything from public-university slots to federal highway contracts.

Last year on ABC News, Obama spoke on a personal level: "I think that my daughters should probably be treated by any admissions officer as folks who are pretty advantaged." He likes this line well enough to have repeated it since. Yet the reality of racial preferences in college enrollments is that they promote those minority applicants who should need the least amount of uplift. In their 1998 book *The Shape of the River*, William G. Bowen and Derek Bok reported that 86 percent of black students admitted to selective colleges come from either middle-class or upper-class backgrounds. What's more, Theodore O'Neill, the undergraduate-admissions director at Obama's former employer (the University of Chicago), told the *Wall Street Journal* that he simply doesn't care. He heard the candidate's request and said that he would still give the Obama girls "a break." For all of Obama's reasonable rhetoric, it appears that little would change in practice.

Racial preferences aren't a voting issue for most people. Yet race has found a few unexpected perches in the election. Hillary Clinton took a great deal of flak when she equated the civil-rights contributions of LBJ and MLK. When the McCain campaign aired a commercial that likened Obama's celebrity status to that of Paris Hilton, it faced charges of race-baiting. A couple of times, Obama has introduced the topic deliberately, such as when he predicted what those nasty Republicans would say of him: "He doesn't look like all those other presidents on those dollar bills" (i.e., he isn't a white guy).

Much will ride on how deftly McCain handles the inevitable eruptions of the race issue between now and November. But he shouldn't shy away from raising the question of racial preferences. He's moving to the side of colorblindness, and represents the broad American mainstream while his opponent sticks with outworn policies that most voters reject. McCain is on the winning side of this one. He should act like it.

FAKE
OBAMA

August 18, 2008

'Hear Me, Earthlings!'

Citizen Obama addresses the world

By Jonah Goldberg

The joke about Pat Buchanan's 1992 Republican National Convention speech was that "it was better in the original German." It's tempting to assume that Barack Obama's Berlin speech was better in the original Esperanto. Speaking near the Brandenburg Gate, Obama proclaimed that he was visiting Berlin not as a politician, but as a "proud citizen of the United States" and—this is the telling part—as a "fellow citizen of the world." (That's *sampatriano de la mondo* in Esperanto, for those interested.) Ronald Reagan used the same phrase, but there are no "citizens of the world." Citizenship requires a state, and unless the United Nations has started issuing passports for all earthlings (can you imagine the lines at the office?), the world has no citizens.

It's tempting to dismiss Obama's Berlin speech as a gassy concatenation of sophomoric platitudes. The trouble is that this vision of world history—and the world's future—wasn't read by a postcolonial-studies major at Ithaca College, from a text illuminated by a lava lamp, with rhetorical flourishes punctuated by bong hits. It was delivered to a throng of some 200,000 adoring, glassy-eyed people by the presumptive presidential nominee of the Democratic party. The Obama campaign billed the speech as a natural continuation of Berlin speeches by JFK and Reagan, two similarly gifted orators who at the time of their own speeches had the added advantage of actually being president, with reason to speak in Berlin more substantial than that they happened to be passing through. Meanwhile, a sycophantic global press corps hyped Obama's speech, before and after, as something akin to an inaugural address from the first President of Planet Earth.

That this was no dorm-room discourse is in one sense a good thing, since Obama's history of the Cold War was not the sort of thing you'd expect from anyone with even a little college history under his belt. In the senator's telling, the Soviet Union was not defeated in a twilight struggle between billions of people; rather, it was defeated by global unity. The lesson of the Berlin Wall's collapse, according to Obama: "There is no challenge too great for a world that stands as one."

This is a bit like saying the lesson of the Crusades has something to do with the redemptive power of interfaith bingo nights. Were the millions of avowed Communists not part of the world? How about the belligerents in Korea and Vietnam, to cite just two of the many proxy wars during that age of global unity? And the billions who formed the Non-Aligned bloc? Or the numerous states that bartered their allegiance with the West and the Soviets—were they part of this global unity? What of the hordes of left-wing activists and agitators here in the United States who blamed America first, last, and always? The Sane Freezers who took to the streets of Berlin to denounce America, not the Soviet Union? How about Obama's friend, former Weatherman terrorist William Ayers? Didn't he plot bombings of American—not Soviet—troops? With unity like this, one shudders to wonder what divisiveness might have looked like.

Obama's blithe revisionism is similar to Bill Clinton's famous claim in 1993 that Americans were unified during the Cold War. "We had an intellectually coherent thing," he effused. "The American people knew what the rules were." Clinton even joked, "Gosh, I miss the Cold War"—because things were so much easier during that time of consensus and unity. This, of course, was the man who described the war in Vietnam as "a war I opposed and despised with a depth of feeling I have reserved solely for racism in America."

But you have to give Bill Clinton some credit. Even in his gauzy fiction, there was still a Cold *War*. It was still America and her allies against an actual enemy, fighting for something. In Obama's telling the Cold War was a universal human endeavor, the whole world united for the sake of unity, hopeful in the cause of . . . hope. We tore down "walls"— real and figurative, or figuratively real—and now the world is threatened again, not by bad people but by those terrible walls. Not real walls, like the barrier that once stood in Berlin, but the even more frightening metaphorical ones. "The greatest danger," Obama declared, is not terrorism or global warming or even nuclear war. No, the "greatest danger of all is to allow new walls to divide us from one another." Then he added: "The walls between old allies on either side of the Atlantic cannot stand. The walls between the countries with the most and those with the least cannot stand. The walls between races and tribes, natives and immigrants, Christian and Muslim and Jew cannot stand. These now are the walls we must tear down."

Okay, so: Walls are bad according to Barack Obama. Got it. Of course, when Obama talks of walls, he often sounds like he's really talking about differences—differences between nations, peoples, religions, and their not-always-harmonious interests. But these differences are real. Tear down the walls between Israelis and Palestinians and you won't have peace; you'll have a lot of dead Israelis or dead Palestinians, or both. Dismantle all distinctions between natives and immigrants, and sovereignty—along with real citizenship—evaporates.

Reagan's universalism was of a different sort, and his argument was that liberty is not a uniquely American possession: "And tonight, we declare anew to our fellow citizens of the world: Freedom is not the sole prerogative of a chosen few; it is the universal right of all God's children." Reagan's universalism was a mark of confidence in American values. In Obama's rhetoric, by contrast, you hear a deeply romantic cosmopolitanism: He says the world won't tolerate our eating to our hearts' content and air-conditioning our homes as we please, and argues that we should stop caring whether immigrants learn English and instead make sure our kids learn Spanish. He has agonized like Prufrock ("Do I dare?") over whether to wear a flag pin. His presumptuous and quickly withdrawn mock presidential seal had no room for *E pluribus unum*. He explained to San Francisco fat-cats that rural Americans bitterly "cling" to their bizarre rituals, unnecessary weapons, and ancient sky god, all because they've been left out on globalization. There are many problems with the worldview that these statements bring into focus. Let us concentrate on three.

First, there's what could be called Obama's arrogant Manichaeism. "My rival in this race," he said early in 2007, "is not other candidates. It's cynicism." Cynics are, naturally, those who disagree with Barack

Obama. Again and again, he dismisses critics and criticism by castigating "divisiveness." Then there's his slogan "We are the ones we've been waiting for," part of his persistently messianic rhetoric, which seems to suggest that those who are not onboard are not just divisive, but unanointed: the ones we haven't been waiting for. Obama himself is never "divisive" for disagreeing with people. "Us" are those who rally to Obama the Unifier; "them" are forever the divisive ones. (Perhaps the GOP should adopt the slogan: "We Are the Ones You're Tired Of.") In short, Obama leads the bridge builders in the glorious struggle against the wall builders.

Second, what about those walls? It's not surprising, given how recycled it all sounded to Americans who've been paying attention, that much of Obama's Berlin rhetoric was merely an extension of his obsession with unity for its own sake, as though this were the highest good. But not only is unity between nation-states not the same thing as unity between individuals, unity for its own sake in foreign affairs has led to cataclysmic confrontations (see "World War I"). Moreover, if the "greatest danger" we face is the possibility of "new walls," then the upshot of Obamism is that the War on Terror—or, if it's more your style, a War on Climate Change—must take a backseat to the more pressing War on Walls. Such a foreign policy would entrench the liberal fetish for collective action: Remember John Kerry's "global test"? The overarching principle of Democratic foreign policy seems to be that it's better to be wrong in a group than to be right alone.

Third, Obama the Cosmopolitan seems to have a real problem distinguishing between the domestic and international spheres. If in his ideal world there would be no "walls" between foreigners and citizens, between Country A and Country B, then why have anything like nations in the first place? If we're all citizens of the world, what is the point of being a citizen of anyplace else? He speaks not of America's burdens, but of the burdens of global citizenship.

Already, Obama has made it clear that his view of the Constitution is entirely open, and can be molded to whatever conception of justice fires the hearts and illuminates the minds of transnational progressives. He says he agrees "with Justice Breyer's view of the Constitution—that it is not a static but rather a living document, and must be read in the context of an ever-changing world." That's one reason Breyer is the Supreme Court's leading advocate of invoking foreign laws—even foreign polls—to glean the Constitution's latest meaning. Obama has also confessed that his foremost criterion for selecting judges will be that they have "the heart, the empathy, to recognize what it's like to be a young teenage mom, the empathy to understand what it's like to be poor or African-American or gay or disabled or old—and that's the criteria by which I'm going to be selecting my judges." Given such a standard, how difficult would it be to add empathy for fellow citizens of the world who, by no more than an accident of birth, aren't citizens of the United States? (Not too hard, it seems, given Obama's enthusiastic support for granting constitutional rights to foreign terrorists captured abroad and held outside the United States.)

All of this might be defensible, even laudable, if it were the musings of a philosopher describing the best possible world. But we aren't electing a philosopher; we're electing a commander-in-chief who is supposed to be a zealous defender of our nation, our Constitution, and our interests—in the world in which we live. There's nothing wrong, and much that is right, in trying to do good for the rest of that world, in whole or in part. But it would be nice if Obama could make it clear he understands that that's a fringe benefit of being president, not the first line of the job description.

September 29, 2008

Hardly

The Democratic nominee is no latter-day Lincoln

By Allen C. Guelzo

H*e is a lawyer from Illinois. He has served in the state legislature, then briefly in Congress, where he has made a name
for himself by opposing an unpopular war. He is lanky and
eloquent and . . .*

So goes the Obama-turns-out-to-be-just-like-Lincoln riff, which
we've been hearing so much of lately. Vote for Obama and we'll get
Lincoln, say commentators like Ken Burns, who thinks Obama's "moral
courage" and "unironic posture" make him Lincolnesque.

The same message emanates from Tony Kushner, whom Steven
Spielberg has tagged to write the screenplay for his forthcoming Lincoln
movie. "The Obama-Lincoln links are real," Kushner told *New York*
magazine's Tim Murphy. Both demonstrate a genius for "reducing dis-
cord and inspiring people to find common ground." And Al Gore, speaking to the Democratic National Convention, also saw in Obama a new
Lincoln, "a clear thinker and great orator" who would shoulder aside the
"50-year lease on the Republican party" held by "big oil and coal."

But the most nuanced celebration of the Obama-Lincoln connection
came in the May 1 *New York Review of Books*, where Garry Wills, author
of the Pulitzer Prize-winning *Lincoln at Gettysburg*, drew a detailed parallel between the ways Lincoln and Obama disarmed their conservative
critics. "Their crippling connection with extremists" unfairly tarred both
men. Lincoln had the abolitionist John Brown, who led the
Pottawatomie Massacre and the Harpers Ferry raid; Obama has Jeremiah
Wright.

In 1859, "extremists" raised "a general panic over John Brown" and applied "the politics of fear" to paint Lincoln as the real extremist. So did modern-day "extremists" over Jeremiah Wright, laying an updated coating of the politics of fear on Barack Obama. Lincoln shrewdly distanced himself from Brown's actions without condemning his cause. And Obama, likewise, "denounced the specific statements of Wright that were indefensible" without letting go of "the concern for the community that Wright had shown." Obama may not have been quite up to the rhetorical bar of "the resplendent Lincoln," Wills admitted, but "what is of lasting interest is their similar strategy for meeting the charge of extremism."

No wonder Ken Burns marveled, as the *Washington Post* paraphrased, that "history may be repeating itself" (and not, we presume, just in syndication). What American, after all, would *not* vote for Abraham Lincoln if he had the chance? "That's the logic that underlies the Obama campaign," concluded Berkeley blogger Bob Burnett. Vote for Obama and you will "elect Lincoln; he'll bring us together."

But is it true?

What is odd about the Obama-Lincoln connection is that the first person to deny it has been Barack Obama. In a piece he wrote in 2005 for a special Lincoln-themed issue of *Time* magazine, Obama looked "in Lincoln's eyes," and what he saw there did not suit him very well. "As I look at his picture," Obama wrote, "I cannot swallow whole the view of Lincoln as the Great Emancipator. As a law professor and civil rights lawyer and as an African American, I am fully aware of his limited views on race. Anyone who actually reads the Emancipation Proclamation knows it was more a military document than a clarion call for justice. Scholars tell us too that Lincoln wasn't immune from political considerations and that his temperament could be indecisive and morose."

Although Obama hailed "Lincoln's rise from poverty, his ultimate mastery of language and law, his capacity to overcome personal loss and remain determined in the face of repeated defeat" as matters that reminded him "of my own struggles," these are characteristics that can be found in William McKinley as easily as in Lincoln. On the points that, so to speak, make Lincoln *Lincoln*—emancipation, the preservation of the Union—Obama found little that looked like Obama.

Obama's instincts were not misplaced. Yes, Lincoln was born in poverty and transformed himself by his own energies. But he never attended a prep school like Obama's Punahou, nor Columbia University, nor Harvard Law School. Nor was Lincoln's grandmother (whom he never knew) a bank vice president, as was Madelyn Dunham.

Yes, Lincoln struggled to educate himself and make a career out of politics, and like Obama he was furious at the ease with which the privileged were handed life on a silver platter. But Lincoln's solution was to encourage entrepreneurship. "I want every man to have the chance—and I believe a black man is entitled to it—in which he can better his condition—when he may look forward and hope to be a hired laborer this year and the next, work for himself afterward, and finally to hire men to work for him! That is the true system." Lincoln's models were Henry Clay (and Clay's "American System" of economic development) and John Stuart Mill, and he frankly endorsed leaving "each man free to acquire property as fast as he can." Lincoln did "not propose any war upon capital"; what he proposed was to "allow the humblest man an equal chance to get rich with everybody else." Obama's models were Malcolm X and Saul Alinsky, and his ultimate goal is not to ensure equal opportunity, but "to ensure fairness."

Yes, Lincoln was a state legislator and lawyer from Illinois, like Obama. But Lincoln quickly became the floor leader for his party and moved to passage the most sweeping economic initiatives ever undertaken in Illinois; Obama led nothing and voted "present" nearly 130 times. Obama's career as a lawyer lasted only two years, from 1993 (when he joined the firm of Davis, Miner, Barnhill & Galland) to 1995 (when he ran for the state senate). Lincoln's law practice stretched over 23 years and over 5,600 cases, and was heavily focused on the protection of property rights, not "community organization." He acted as counsel and lobbyist for the Illinois Central Railroad in the 1850s, representing it at least 50 times between 1853 and 1859 and earning a reputation for honesty. Obama's brief association with DMB&G is probably best known today because of the firm's most notorious client, Tony Rezko.

Yes, critics tagged Lincoln with the dark badge of John Brown, and yes, Lincoln neatly sidestepped the issue while remaining focused on opposing the spread of slavery. But unlike Obama and Rezko, Lincoln had never met Brown, had not sat with Brown in church for 20 years, and had not allowed Brown to baptize his children. Nor did Lincoln have political ties to Brown comparable to Obama's ties to Weather Underground terrorist Bill Ayers.

Lincoln condemned Brown as the sort of "enthusiast" who "broods over the oppression of a people till he fancies himself commissioned by Heaven to liberate them." Even if Brown "agreed with us in thinking slavery wrong," Lincoln also said, "that cannot excuse violence, bloodshed, and treason." John Brown was not nearly the problem for Lincoln that Jeremiah Wright and Bill Ayers will prove to be for Barack Obama.

I will happily admit that there *are* resemblances between Barack Obama and Abraham Lincoln. But then, I can claim to resemble Lincoln, too—in that I have two ears, a nose, and so forth. This is, of course, superficial—just as most historical resemblances turn out to be superficial.

Comparing Obama to Lincoln would have meaning only if Obama were facing a specific national crisis—one that had built for 30 years, been galvanized by regional political blocs, and threatened to result in war, the breakup of the Union, and violent assaults on federal military installations.

But if by "resemblance" we mean to speak about shared ideas, then it is hard to think of two American presidential candidates more dissimilar to each other than Obama and Lincoln. "The legitimate object of government," said Lincoln, is only "to do for a community of people whatever they need to have done but cannot do at all, or cannot so well do, for themselves. . . . In all that the people can individually do as well for themselves, government ought not to interfere."

When that becomes Obama's philosophy, we can start talking about the second coming of Abraham Lincoln.

February 23, 2009

Our Lincoln

Obama, he was not

By Allen C. Guelzo

'**W**hat is conservatism?"
This question has been getting more than its usual
share of raking over in the post-Bush beginnings of
2009. But it was being asked in terms just as blunt 150 years ago, and
the man asking the question was Abraham Lincoln.

Fresh from his near-victory over Stephen Douglas for a U.S. Senate
seat from Illinois, and soon to deliver a headline-grabbing speech at New
York City's Cooper Union, Lincoln posed the question to a political rally
in Leavenworth, Kan., in December 1859.

In the broadest sense, said Lincoln, conservatism meant "preserving
the old against the new." In the American context, it meant holding the
Union together—a determination to "stick to, contend for" the
Constitution as "adopted by our fathers who framed the government
under which we live." And in the supercharged atmosphere of the late
1850s, with the slaveholding states of the South threatening to break up
the Constitution and the Union, conservatism meant nominating for
president "a national conservative man, unhackneyed by political ter-
giversations and . . . fresh from the people." Such a conservative president would have not only to think conservatively, but to act conservatively. Despite his deep opposition to the spread of slavery in the United
States, Lincoln was not "in favor of the exercise of" presidential power
against it "unless upon some conservative principle."

Still, Lincoln knew his conservatism would be misrepresented—or
simply ignored—by a press eager to paint him as an extremist. "If I were
to labor a month, I could not express my conservative views and intentions more clearly and strongly, than they are expressed," Lincoln wrote
irritably to the editor of the *Louisville Journal* a week before his election

as president. "And yet even you, who do occasionally speak of me in terms of personal kindness, give no prominence to these oft repeated expressions of conservative views and intentions."

Lincoln would probably be just as irritated to see how routinely those "oft repeated expressions of conservative views and intentions" are still being given "no prominence" on his 200th birthday. On February 12, the Abraham Lincoln Bicentennial Commission, whose board of directors is top-heavy with Democratic politicos, will sponsor a "National Teach-In" on Lincoln—featuring three liberal Democrats. The Lincoln Group of the District of Columbia will host a banquet that evening whose main speaker will be George McGovern. And a companion volume to the Library of Congress's new Lincoln exhibition features commentaries on famous Lincoln documents by Toni Morrison, Jimmy Carter, Gore Vidal, Mario Cuomo, Tony Kushner, Sen. Dick Durbin, Bill Clinton, and Ken Burns (as well as Lew Lehrman, William Safire, George H. W. Bush, George W. Bush, and Newt Gingrich, but the liberals easily outnumber the conservatives).

Not surprisingly, Lincoln's declaration in Columbus, Ohio, in September 1859—that the "chief and real purpose of the Republican party is eminently conservative" and "proposes nothing save and except to restore this government to its original tone . . . and there to maintain it, looking for no further change . . . than that which the original framers of the government themselves expected and looked forward to"—is not one of the book's featured documents.

Still, if Lincoln's bicentennial laurels are not being plucked from conservative trees, this is not through any fault of Lincoln's. From his earliest political stirrings in the 1830s, Lincoln was a torchbearer for free markets, individual liberty and economic mobility, the rule of law, natural rights, and prudence in governing. He had no Caesarian notion of the powers of the presidency, no use for what we today call "diversity" politics. Yet he achieved the presidency in 1861, just in time to find himself facing a national crisis that changed all the ground rules by which he expected to put those ideas into play.

At the core of Lincoln's conservatism was the Declaration of Independence. He said he had "never had a feeling politically that did not spring from the sentiments embodied in the Declaration of

Independence," and he gave short shrift to the agrarian or aristocratic Toryism of the Calhoun or Metternich school. In particular, he regarded Jefferson's key sentence—"We hold these truths to be self-evident, that all men are created equal, that they are endowed by their Creator with certain unalienable Rights, that among these are Life, Liberty and the pursuit of Happiness"—as the "proposition" to which the American republic had been "dedicated" at its birth.

This was not a proposition confected only by Americans for the unique circumstances of America; *created equal* was a statement of natural law, "applicable to all men and all times." If asked to surrender or compromise that proposition, Lincoln said with eerie prescience shortly before his inauguration in 1861, he would prefer to "be assassinated on this spot." At the same time, though, the proposition owed nothing to the Jacobin spirit of radical egalitarianism. Lincoln's notion of equality was about leveling up, not whittling down.

Equality meant abolishing artificial aristocratic privilege and opening up the starting line in life to everyone, regardless of who his parents were, what his religion was, or what his race happened to be. The promise embodied by the Declaration was "that in due time the weights should be lifted from the shoulders of all men, and that all should have an equal chance." When the Civil War came, he interpreted it as "a struggle for maintaining in the world, that form, and substance of government, whose leading object is, to elevate the condition of men—to lift artificial weights from all shoulders—to clear the paths of laudable pursuit for all—to afford all, an unfettered start, and a fair chance, in the race of life."

The practical purpose of equality was twofold: to create an equal voice for all the governed in their government, and to create an environment, social and economic, in which self-improvement and social mobility could operate freely. "Advancement," Lincoln declared, "improvement in condition—is the order of things in a society of equals." Legalizing slavery represented an unnatural intervention of government into the marketplace, conferring unfair labor advantages on white slave-owners at the expense of black slaves and poor white farmers alike. The slave had the product of his labor stolen out of his hands; the farmer could not stand up economically to the vast economies of scale enjoyed by the thousand-bale planters. "Advancement" and "improvement" for both evaporated.

Lincoln's best example of advancement was himself. "Twenty-five years ago, I was a hired laborer," Lincoln said in March 1860. He was little better than "a slave." But in the unbound atmosphere of "a society of equals," he had made himself free—"so free that they let me practice law." And so it was for everyone else in "a society of equals." Equality was the friend of talent, and the enemy of entitlement.

Lincoln understood that equality of opportunity was not a guarantee of "fairness" of result. "Some will get wealthy," he conceded, but that was no excuse for class complaint or class warfare. "I don't believe in a law to prevent a man from getting rich; it would do more harm than good." His theory of the ideal economy was one where "the prudent, penniless beginner in the world, labors for wages awhile, saves a surplus with which to buy tools or land, for himself; then labors on his own account another while, and at length hires another new beginner to help him." He never blamed poverty on an unfeeling capitalist machine, nor, for that matter, did he try to wear the poverty of his youth as a badge of pride.

His father, Thomas Lincoln, was an ignorant farmer who (according to one semi-literate neighbor) "Jest Raised a Nuf for his own use" and shunned participation in the newly emerging market economy of the 19th century for anything more than "his Shugar and Coffee and Such Like." Abraham Lincoln, however, was initiated into the world of cash markets on the day two men hurriedly hired the boy to take them on his raft midstream into the Ohio River to catch a passing steamer. Each man tossed him "a silver half-dollar," and while this might seem "like a trifle," Lincoln thought "it was a most important incident in my life." He had learned how labor could be converted into capital. "The world seemed wider and fairer before me," he recalled, "I was a more hopeful and thoughtful boy from that time."

Lincoln had hardly turned 21 when he bid the farm—and "the backside of the world"—goodbye. He turned to the larger world of commerce, going into business first as a clerk and then as a proprietor in two stores in New Salem, the up-and-coming *entrepôt* of central Illinois. He failed, as did New Salem. But without much pause, Lincoln plunged himself into the study of law, which (in the memorable phrase of Charles Grier Sellers) enlisted him among "the shock troops of capitalism." From the time he was admitted to the central-Illinois bar in 1837 until he became president in 1861, Lincoln managed a sprawling legal practice—some 5,600 cases and over a hundred thousand documents. Only 194 of them were criminal cases; the bulk of his practice was civil and commercial, most of it involving debt collections, bankruptcies, and land disputes. By the 1850s, his most frequent and lucrative clients were the Illinois railroads. He did not at all mind foreclosing delinquent mortgages or writing lengthy opinions for the Illinois Central Railroad on how to evict squatters from railroad land. As Henry Clay Whitney, another central-Illinois lawyer, admitted, "I never found him unwilling to appear in behalf of a great 'soulless corporation.'"

Having built himself up from being "a strange, friendless, uneducated, penniless boy, working on a flat boat," Lincoln had no desire "to propose any war upon capital." If anything, he said, he wanted "to allow the humblest man an equal chance to get rich with everybody else" and "leave each man free to acquire property as fast as he can." Lincoln had little sympathy for those who complained that the competitive workings of a market economy were impersonal or greedy. "Free labor"—a man's right to choose his own work, take risks, and reap the rewards, benefiting the community along with himself—was actually "the just and generous, and prosperous system, which opens the way for all—gives hope to all, and energy, and progress, and improvement of condition to all." When people failed in their "chance" to rise, "it is not the fault of the system, but because of either a dependent nature which prefers it, or improvidence, folly, or singular misfortune."

In case of such a failure, the only solution—apart from calling in the forces of privilege and favoritism to put an end to equality—was to allow a free market to correct itself or allow an unsuccessful striver the freedom to make a second try. "Some of you will be successful," he told the Wisconsin State Agricultural Society in 1859; "others will be disappointed, and will be in a less happy mood." For them, Lincoln's only advice was "the maxim, 'Better luck next time'; and then, by renewed exertion, make that better luck for themselves." When he was asked by a young schoolteacher for advice about studying law, he wrote back, "obtaining a thorough knowledge of the law . . . is very simple, though laborious, and tedious. . . . Work, work, work, is the main thing."

But the promise of self-improvement was only one corollary of equality, and it might turn out to be empty unless it was accompanied by equal liberty and an equal voice for all the governed in their government. For this reason, it was the hooting shame of America that while it talked of equality and free labor, it legalized the enslavement and dehumanization of blacks. "When one starts poor, as most do in the race of life, free society is such that he knows he can better his condition," Lincoln argued; "he knows that there is no fixed condition of labor, for his whole life." But slavery fixed an entire category of human beings in precisely that hopeless situation, politically and economically, on no basis other than color. For that reason alone, Lincoln was "naturally anti slavery. If slavery is not wrong, nothing is wrong."

As the "one retrograde institution in America," slavery turned Americans into "political hypocrites before the world." Just as bad, by allowing one man to own the fruits of another man's labor, it discouraged hard work in both. In this way, slavery was turning labor from the path of self-improvement into the lot of the debased and dispirited. The ownership of slaves "betokened not only the possession of wealth but indicated the gentleman of leisure who was above and scorned labour," and only encouraged the "giddy headed young men who looked upon work as vulgar and ungentlemanly."

Above all, however, slavery was a violation of natural law, because a man's right to "eat the bread, without leave of anybody else, which his own hand earns" was indissolubly linked with the natural right to liberty that Jefferson had recognized in every human creature (and that made Jefferson uneasy about the slaves he himself owned). Anyone who stopped his ears and tried to pretend that blacks were excluded from that natural right was "blowing out the moral lights around us . . . and eradicating the light of reason and the love of liberty in this American people."

Slavery's defenders made the pretense of blacks' exclusion easier to maintain by manipulating the language of liberty to their own ends. Liberty became the "right" to own slaves. Slaves became "property" to be defended, as though human chattels were no different from donkeys or pigs. And the decision of any majority on any subject—including who might be the best candidates for enslavement—was construed as the essence of democracy. "The doctrine of self government is right—absolutely and eternally right," Lincoln said. But "if the negro is a man, is it not to that extent, a total destruction of self-government, to say that he too shall not govern himself?" There was a line that even the power of majorities could not cross, a line drawn by nature and nature's God that no amount of talk about "choice" could ever really efface.

Slavery had to be dealt with, but within the constraints of the Constitution and the rule of law. Americans must be "ever true to Liberty," but also true to "the Union, and the Constitution—true to Liberty, not selfishly, but upon principle—not for special classes of men, but for all men, true to the union and the Constitution, as the best means to advance that liberty."

His belief in the 1850s was that the "best means" to ensure the demise of slavery was to confine it to the southern states, where it had long been legal, and prevent its spread into the western territories. Locked into the South, slavery would eventually asphyxiate, as slave-based cotton agriculture used up the resources of the southern soils. Even then, the emancipation of the slaves would have to involve "three main features—gradual—compensation—and vote of the people" in order to ensure its political legitimacy and provide time to create "some practical system by which the two races could gradually live themselves out of their old relation to each other, and both come out better prepared for the new."

A civil war was not part of Lincoln's list of possible solutions to the slavery controversy. But civil war was thrust upon him, and the war put into his hands, as commander-in-chief. Yet even the presidential war powers, which he used to issue the Emancipation Proclamation, had to be handled with restraint. When his cabinet urged him to expand the scope of the Proclamation, he demurred: If he based emancipation on anything except the "military necessity" that his war powers authorized, "would I not thus give up all footing upon constitution or law? Would I not thus be in the boundless field of absolutism?" He never saw himself as a crusader, licensed to strike down injustice with a righteous flail. When George Hay Stuart of the U.S. Christian Commission congratulated Lincoln on the abolition of slavery, wrote an early biographer, "Mr. Lincoln replied in a few, short clear words, 'My Friends: you owe me no gratitude for what I have done. . . . I trust that this has all been for us a work of *duty*.'"

For all the complaining about Lincoln's exercise of the war powers and his suspension of habeas corpus, the actual volume of military arrests and trials was small. And for all the complaining that Lincoln used the war to expand the powers of the federal government to an unconstitutional degree, the expansion was never more than a utilitarian device for meeting the unprecedented demands of 19th-century war-making. (The federal government began shrinking back to only 4 percent of its wartime peak within days of the news of Appomattox.) The massive federal bureaucracy that so antagonizes conservatives today was the creation of the 20th century—and especially of Woodrow Wilson, Franklin Roosevelt, and Lyndon Johnson—not of Abraham Lincoln. The notion of "affirmative action," of nationalized health care, of "comparable worth" litigation and the wholesale release of terrorist detainees would have reduced him to splutters.

If to love liberty, to hate slavery, and to believe that free labor holds out the best hope of "self-improvement" and "advancement" do *not* exemplify what American conservatism ought to be, then I am at a loss to know what does. Nor can I imagine what would offer better proof of Lincoln's conservative credentials than his advocacy of procedural equality, freedom, and an open society. What I do know is that the same voices that twisted liberty into "choice" and clamored for privilege and security rather than openness and mobility have not changed all that much since they were raised in defense of slavery.

The politics of race and blood, and the culture of hedonism and the unbridled personal will, serve inevitably to plant "the seeds of despotism around your own doors." For Lincoln, moral principle, as captured in the Declaration of Independence and in natural law, is all, or almost all, that unites us, and all that ensures that *this nation under God, shall have a new birth of freedom, and that government of the people, by the people, for the people, shall not perish from the earth.*

If those words were his only banner, they would still be enough to show that he is yet our Lincoln.

Message: I'm Insecure

What the President's oil-spill blunder revealed about him

By Rob Long

Rule One of great acting is, Do not read the stage directions.

You don't, for instance, wrap up Hamlet's big Act Two soliloquy—". . . the play's the thing / Wherein I'll catch the conscience of the King"—and then say "Exit."

Years ago, during the George H. W. Bush administration, public-opinion surveys began to register a troubling trend for a president campaigning for reelection: More and more people felt that Bush just didn't care about people's suffering during the (fairly shallow) recession of the early 1990s.

You've got to send them the message that you care, they told him. So, dutifully, in his next big public outing, he tried to send the message to the voters that he cared. He wound up a boilerplate stump speech by declaring, with as much passion as he could muster, "Message: I care!"

No, no, Mr. President, you could imagine his advisers saying. *The "message" part is for us, it's an internal thing. You're supposed to give them the message that you care. By showing that you care.*

Right, he might have replied, *I did that. How much clearer could I have been?*

You're not supposed to say the "message" part, they might have replied as the presidential limo sped away.

But it says right here on the talking-points card you gave me, he could have shouted back. *Right here! "Message: I care!"*

But by that time, a pudgy governor of Arkansas had already bit his lower lip, felt our pain, and made us temporarily ignore his brittle wife. That was a guy who understood Rule One.

The truth was, Bush really didn't care. The 1990–91 recession was almost over by the time he started getting walloped in the polls, before someone had handed him a memo titled "Messaging That Bush Cares" or something equally futile. Unemployment, slow growth, these things had already started turning around. There was nothing for him to do. And as all grownups know, recessions happen.

But saying "Message: I care!" captured all of the loose threads out in the crazytown of public opinion and braided them together into part of the rope that ended up hanging the first Bush administration.

Twenty years later, everyone seems to be exercised over President Obama's recent declaration that his big project, when confronting the massive, gushing BP oil spill in the Gulf of Mexico, is to figure out "whose ass to kick."

Talking to Matt Lauer on NBC's *Today* show, our skinny president said the following deeply Freudian thing: "I don't sit around just talking to experts because this is a college seminar. We talk to these folks because they potentially have the best answers—so I know whose ass to kick."

I'm not as interested as the rest of the world is, I guess, in the "whose ass to kick" part of the declaration. *Show more emotion*, I'm sure Obama's advisers have been saying to him since the oil started to gush. *Be more passionate. Send people the message that you care.* And so he did— absurdly, but that's what happens to presidents when they hit the oil slick. At least he didn't say, "Message: I'm going to kick some ass."

Here's the part I find the most interesting: "I don't sit around just talking to experts because this is a college seminar." This from the former professor who ran a health-care-reform summit meeting like the cranky chairman of a faculty committee at a third-rate college. Who finds it impossible to describe something as simple and clear as Islamic fundamentalism without weasel-wording equivocation. Who, in other words, thinks this is a college seminar.

I am not, let me stipulate at the outset, a licensed psychiatrist. My understanding of the works of Sigmund Freud are cursory—college psychology class; skimmed the reading, bluffed my way through the exam—and it pains me to admit that I am, still, not legally allowed to prescribe drugs.

But I know the basics. I know that we get weird in the pre-verbal stage of development. I know that we have malignant egos. I know that we end up marrying the closest approximation to our most complicated parent. And I know that when we say things, we often inadvertently reveal the truth about ourselves. A Freudian slip, for example, is when we say one thing when we mean a mother. Another. You know what I mean.

When a person—especially someone as tightly wound as our president—emphatically declares something that sounds a little too specific, watch out. He's not making a point; he's reading the stage directions. He's telling you what he's afraid you think of him, and he's often correct.

Psychiatrists love this little trick, because it makes their work so incredibly easy. You just wait for the patient to say something weird about himself, and you pounce. Voters do the same thing. When George H. W. Bush tried to show voters the scale of his caring by barking, "Message: I care!" they all suddenly saw the president of the United States stretched out on a Mies daybed, and they scribbled in their notebooks, "Patient seems concerned re: not caring impression. Patient may lack proper sympathy."

But psychiatrists don't fire patients—not at $300 per session. Voters, on the other hand, positively relish it.

All of this is a little unfair, of course. A president who spent his entire working life in either a crackpot left-wing nonprofit or a law school—although when you say it like that, it's hard to tell the difference—couldn't be expected to know anything about the complexities of deep-water drilling, the physics of oil under pressure, the trajectory of an oil slick as it slimes its way to shore.

So, yes, it's easy to imagine that there's been a bit of the college seminar going on there, in the Oval Office.

But why so defensive? Or, as we might have scribbled in our notebooks as President Obama took his place on the couch: "Patient v. v. defensive re: lack of oil knowledge. Ego bruise? Anger due to inflated sense of self vs. inability to stop oil leak? Anger due to sense of self under fire from oil leak, voters, etc.? Sense that like college seminar, he is all talk, no action?"

All of which is accurate. And all of which seems to be what voters are thinking.

Especially when he added, gratuitously, that he wanted to know "whose ass to kick," when everyone knew that what he really meant was "whose ass to sue," which doesn't sound very butch.

It's been said that the Deepwater Horizon oil spill is Obama's Katrina, but that's really not accurate. It's Obama's "Message: I care" moment. It's when he started to read the stage directions.

A brilliant actor once told me that the hardest thing to play is drunk. And then he told me how to do it.

You play not drunk. You don't play a guy weaving and slurring and bumping into stuff. You play a guy consciously, deliberately, carefully not doing any of those things. The way you indicate how immensely incapacitated you are, in other words, is to act super, super sober, to declare, in other words, that not only are you not drunk, you're the opposite of drunk. Which just makes you seem incredibly drunk.

Audiences find this hilarious. Voters, well, we shall see.

SIDEKICK
OBAMA

April 21, 2008

Mrs. Obama's America

It's an interesting place—but nowhere we should want to be

By Mark Steyn

Michelle, *ma belle*: These are words that go together well. She looks fabulous, like a presidential spouse out of some dream movie—glossy hair, triple strand of pearls, vaguely retro suits that subtly remind you she'd be the most glamorous first lady since Jackie Kennedy.

Michelle, "fear," "cynicism": These are words that go together more problematically. Mrs. Obama is most famous for declaring, about her husband's candidacy, that "for the first time in my adult lifetime I'm really proud of my country." Just a throwaway line reflecting no more than the narcissism and self-absorption required to mount a presidential campaign in the 21st century? Possibly—were it not for the fact that almost every time the candidate's wife speaks extemporaneously she seems to offer some bon mot consistent with that bleak assessment.

'YOU MUST WORK,' DECLARES DEAR LEADER

And when she stops looking back across the final grim despairing decades of the 20th century ("Life for regular folks has gotten worse over the course of my lifetime") and contemplates the sunlit uplands of the new utopia, it doesn't, tonally, get any cheerier. Pretend for a moment that the name of the candidate had been excised from the following remarks. Would it seem part of the natural discourse of a constitutional republic of citizen legislators? Or does it sound more appropriate to the leadership cult of Basketkhazia or some other one-man stan?

"[INSERT NAME OF MESSIANIC LEADER HERE] will require you to work. He is going to demand that you shed your cynicism. That you put down your divisions. That you come out of your isolation, that you move out of your comfort zone. That you push yourselves to be better. And that you engage. [LEADER] will never allow you to go back to your lives as usual, uninvolved, uninformed."

The above words were his wife's vision of life under the administration of Barack Obama, the transformative presidential candidate offering change you can believe in—or else. I hate to sound like I'm walled up in the Shed of Cynicism, but the constitutional right to be "uninvolved" and "uninformed" is one of the most precious, at least if the alternative is being "required" to work at coming out of your isolation and engaging with fellow members of the uninvolved, uninformed masses as we push ourselves to move out of our comfort zone.

Fortunately, none of that seems to mean anything in real English, though it has the makings of a totalitarian therapeutic rewrite of "Put on a Happy Face":

> Gray skies are gonna push off
> Move out your comfort zone
> Barack will work your tush off
> Move out your comfort zone
> Give up your gloomy lives so uninvolved
> It's not allowed
> Barack requires every one involved
> So join the crowd . . .

I'm willing to cut presidential spouses a lot of slack. When Senator Obama said Jeremiah Wright was like a goofy uncle, it was pointed out that your relatives are a given but you get to choose your pastor. It's true that you also get to choose your wife, but, unless you're particularly farsighted, you don't always choose with a presidential run in mind. I found Teresa Heinz's tone-deafness to the rhythms of democratic politics one of the more charmingly genuine features of John Kerry's phony-baloney populist campaign. Who wouldn't love a woman who, shanghaied into lunching at Wendy's, demands to know what "chili" is and has to have it explained to her by the clerk that it's a meat-based food dish widely consumed around the United States?

Oddly enough, despite being a couple of decades younger and

several gazillion dollars poorer, Mrs. Obama has a tin ear even Mrs. Kerry must marvel at. Addressing a group of struggling women in economically torpid central Ohio, Michelle Obama eschewed the usual I-feel-your-pain shtick and invited her audience to feel hers, lurching into a long riff on the expense of extracurricular activities for her daughters, piano and dance and summer camp, and somehow she and Barack are expected to figure out how to pay for it on a combined salary of 500 grand a year, not including his book royalties and her corporate directorship. (Nor the house they bought for $1.6 million.) Mrs. Obama's plaint was worryingly reminiscent of the time the Prince of Wales, attempting to bond with some of the British Army's black recruits, said that he too knew what it was to suffer prejudice: At his boarding school some of the boys had been prejudiced against him because he was a prince. ("The people in my dormitory are foul," he wrote to the Queen in 1964. "They throw slippers all night long or hit me with pillows.")

You can understand why a visit to Wendy's by Teresa Heinz, a Portuguese Mozambican ketchup heiress, should come off like an ill-advised anthropological expedition, but it's less clear why so much of American life should seem so foreign to Michelle Obama. Come presidential season, the Democrats prefer blind dates while the Republicans make do with the old coot who's been pestering them for a night out since *Gold Diggers of 1935*. So the Dems nominate total unknowns—Carter, Dukakis, Clinton—while the GOP nominates fellows they know only too well—Bush 41, Dole, McCain.

In the case of Barack Obama, it's not just that he's unknown, but that he seems eerily unknowable. When assorted members of the Kennedy clan endorsed him, I was struck by the one respect in which Senator Obama is undoubtedly Kennedyesque: Like JFK, he's cool and a little remote in public; he'll shake hands, he'll kiss babies, he'll essay a self-deprecating remark or two, but that's it. In a white guy, the cool would seem arrogant: Even Jack Kennedy couldn't get away with being Jack Kennedy on the stump in 2008. Yet, next to an oleaginous, ingratiating creep like John Edwards, flaunting his Dickensian childhood, Obama is, like Churchill's Russia, a riddle wrapped in a mystery inside an enigma. And, as with Churchill's Russia, it's not always clear whether the interests of Obama and the United States always coincide. In the youthful chapters of his autobiography, *Dreams of My Father*, Barack deploys terms such as "Eurocentrism" and "post-colonialism" with amused detachment, as if to reassure us that even at college these were only ever drolly ironic concepts to him—or, at any rate, merely the universal passwords to sex and drugs. But the same amused detachment pervades the later chapters. On a recent conference call to discuss debate strategy against Hillary, Mrs. Obama interrupted the high-priced consultants to urge, "Barack! *Feel*—don't think." But it's not apparent what, if anything, Barack does feel.

THE SOULS OF CONFLICTED FOLK

That's where Michelle comes in. Whether or not Senator Obama's friends know him, he doesn't seem to know them, not if Tony Rezko or Jeremiah Wright is anything to go by. After another medley of Jeremiah's Greatest Hits was released, the senator declared: "All of the statements that have been the subject of controversy are ones that I vehemently condemn"—or, as translated by *Slate*'s Mickey Kaus, "If it offends you, I condemn it." The Wright brother flies solo as far as his wilder flights of fancy are concerned. Well, okay. But the problem for the enigmatic Obama is that his wife gives every indication of broadly subscribing to the Reverend Wright's world view, albeit without the profanity and accompanying pelvic thrusts.

She was born in 1964, so, unlike, say, Condi Rice, she has no vivid childhood memories of racial segregation. She grew up in a conventional two-parent household that, though poor and living in a small apartment, gathered each evening for dinner, so she's not a victim of the Great Society's atomization of the black family. She was among the first generation to benefit from "affirmative action," which was supposed to ameliorate the lingering grievances of racism but seems, in Mrs. Obama's case, merely to have transformed them into post-modern pseudo-grievance. "All my life I have confronted people who had a certain expectation of me," she told an audience in Madison. "Every step of the way, there was somebody there telling me what I couldn't do. Applied to Princeton. 'You can't go there, your test scores aren't high enough.' I went. I graduated with departmental honors. And then I wanted to go to

Harvard. And that was probably a little too tough for me. I didn't even know why they said that."

But hang on. Her test scores weren't "high enough" for Princeton. Yet, rather than telling her, "You can't go there," they took her anyway. And all the thanks they get is that her test scores are now a recurring point of resentment: "The stuff that we're seeing in these polls," she told an interviewer, "has played out my whole life. You know, always been told by somebody that I'm not ready, that I can't do something, my scores weren't high enough." If you were, say, Elizabeth Edwards and your scores weren't high enough, that'd be that (Teresa Heinz could probably leverage the whole Mozambican thing). Yet Mrs. Obama regards state-mandated compensation for previous racism as a new burden to bear.

In an early indication of the post-modern narcissism on display at Zanesville, she arrived as a black woman at Princeton and wrote her undergraduate thesis on the problems of being a black woman at Princeton. *Princeton-Educated Blacks and the Black Community* is a self-meditation by the then Miss Robinson on the question of whether an Ivy League black student drawn remorselessly into the white world is betraying lower-class blacks. As she put it:

> A separationist is more likely to have a realistic impression of the plight of the Black lower class because of the likelihood that a separationist is more closely associated with the Black lower class than are integrationist [*sic*]. By actually working with the Black lower class or within their communities as a result of their ideologies, a separationist [*sic*] may better understand the desparation [*sic*] of their situation and feel more hopeless about a resolution as opposed to an integrationist who is ignorant to their plight.

Ah, the benefits of an elite education. The thesis is dopey, illiterate, and bizarrely punctuated, but so are the maunderings of many American students. What makes Miss Robinson's youthful opus relevant is that the contradictions it agonizes over have dominated her life. Indeed, her apparent bitterness at a society that has given her blessings she could not have enjoyed anywhere else on earth seems explicitly to derive from her inability to live either as an "integrationist who is ignorant to [the] plight" of "the Black lower class" or a "separationist" embracing its hopelessness and "desperation." Instead, she rode her privileged education to wealth and success and then felt bad about it. That's why she talks about money—her money—more than any other contender for first lady ever has: It's like an ongoing interior monologue about whether she sold out for too cheap a price. Still, she's learned her lesson. As she told her listeners in Ohio:

"We left corporate America, which is a lot of what we're asking young people to do. Don't go into corporate America."

That's what the Obama campaign is "asking young people to do"? "Don't go into corporate America"? But isn't "corporate America" what pays for, among other things, the Gulf Emir–sized retinue of courtiers the average U.S. senator now travels with?

And in what sense did the Obamas "leave" corporate America? Mrs. Obama works for the University of Chicago Hospitals. She's not a nurse or doctor. She's a lawyer who was taken on by the hospitals in 2002 to run "programs for community relations, neighborhood outreach, volunteer recruitment, staff diversity, and minority contracting." In 2005, she got a $200,000 pay raise and was appointed Vice President for Community and External Affairs and put in charge of managing "the Hospitals' business diversity program."

You can appreciate why Barack Obama is less gung-ho than Hillary for socialized health care. If you work at the Royal Victoria Hospital in Montreal, there are certainly the usual professional diversity apparatchiks, but they're not pulling down 300K a year plus benefits. You need a "corporate sector" for that.

This is what makes Michelle Obama in Zanesville another Teresa Heinz in Wendy's or Prince of Wales making small-talk with black squaddies. Her "adult lifetime" has been spent in some of the most unrepresentative quarters of American life: Princeton, the ever-metastasizing bureaucracy of diversity enforcement, and Jeremiah Wright's neo-segregationist ghetto of Afrocentric liberation theology and conspiracy theory. If young people were to follow the Obamas' message and abandon "corporate America" for the above precincts, the nation would collapse. Michelle Obama embodies a peculiar mix of privilege and victimology, which is not where most Americans live. On the other hand, it does make her a terrific Oprah guest: Unlike her sonorous, dignified, restrained husband, she has exactly the combination of wealth and vulnerability prized by connoisseurs of daytime talk shows.

There's something pitiful about a political culture that has no use for Mitt Romney, a hugely successful businessman, but venerates a woman who gets more than 300 grand for running a "neighborhood outreach" and "staff diversity" program. They seem curious career choices for the closest confidante of a man who claims to be running as a "post-racial" candidate. Which Barack Obama certainly could have been: He's no tired old race-baiter making a lucrative career out of grievance-mongering, like Jesse Jackson, President-for-Life of the Republic of Himself. In many ways, he's similar to Colin Powell, a bipartisan figure born to a British subject (in Powell's case, from the Caribbean; in Obama's, from colonial Kenya) and thus untinged by the bitterness of the African-American experience. And yet the two most important figures in Obama's adult life exemplify all the tired obsessions he was supposed to transcend. I don't agree with Powell on anything very much, from abortion to Iraq. But, with hindsight, it's a tragedy that he didn't have the fire in his belly to run in 1996. He was truly the post-racial candidate Senator Obama poses as.

Most Americans—even those upscale white liberals who embraced Obama as the new black best friend they'd been waiting for all these years—don't want to think about race that much. I don't suppose the Rev. Jeremiah Wright, in his new, 98 percent white gated community, even thinks about it *that* much. And as Michelle Obama advised: *Feel*—don't think. Is it a bumper sticker yet? It ought to be. It gets to the heart of the matter better than "*change you can believe in,*" "*belief you can change,*" "*change you can feel,*" "*hope you can grope,*" or the rest of the pleasantly gaseous uplift. Everyone feels good about Obama. He's the fellow we've wanted to feel good about for so long.

But Michelle Obama, and her own uncertain feelings for America, put a big question mark over that.

May 5, 2008

By His Friends Ye Shall Know Him

The trial of Tony Rezko spells trouble for Barack

By Stephen Spruiell

hicago—Barack Obama has two categories of problematic friends. On one hand, there are the radicals—such people as his pastor, Jeremiah Wright, and his friend Bill Ayers, a former leader in the homegrown '60s terror group the Weather Underground. On the other hand, there are the players—such Illinois political operators as indicted fundraiser and businessman Antoin "Tony" Rezko, a man who raised hundreds of thousands of dollars for Obama's campaigns and helped him buy a $1.65 million house here.

The radicals have received more coverage in the national media so far, simply because the public nature of what they do makes them easier to cover. All a broadcast network needs to do is play clips from Wright's "God damn America" sermon, bring on a couple of political analysts to talk about it, and *voilà*: insta-story. For newspapers, it's as simple as reprinting excerpts from Ayers's memoir, in which he wrote, "Everything was absolutely ideal on the day I bombed the Pentagon."

But Rezko's corruption trial, which has been unfolding in a federal courtroom here over the past several weeks, has the potential to change the balance. For one thing, the trial has already yielded new information on the corrupt activities of several other Illinois players to whom Obama has ties, including his former boss, Allison Davis. For another, Rezko stands a good chance of being convicted when the jury decides this case, which should happen sometime this summer. If he is, it will create a new opening for Obama's opponents and a new opportunity for the press to probe his relationships within the bipartisan political machine that Illinoisans refer to simply as "The Combine."

Rezko's trial has lifted the veil on Illinois's infernally corrupt political establishment, and a government witness named Stuart Levine has taken on the role of a meth-snorting, double-dealing Virgil, guiding the public through it. Levine, a drug addict and crooked GOP operative, is testifying for the government in order to avoid spending the rest of his life in prison. Over the course of seven days of direct examination by the prosecution, he described a statewide network of fraud, extortion, and bribery that included key figures in the administration of Illinois governor Rod Blagojevich, a Democrat.

One of those figures was Tony Rezko, a top fundraiser for and adviser to Blagojevich. Most of the public first heard of Rezko when Hillary Clinton mentioned him during a Democratic debate sponsored by CNN back in January. After Obama criticized Clinton for her ties to Wal-Mart, Clinton shot back with, "I was fighting against [conservative] ideas when you were practicing law and representing your contributor, Rezko, in his slum-landlord business in inner-city Chicago."

Obama responded that, as a young associate at the law firm of Davis Miner Barnhill & Galland, he had done about five hours of work on a real-estate deal involving a "church group" and "this individual" (meaning Rezko), implying that he barely knew the man. In fact, Rezko was one of Obama's first political contacts in Chicago, and the two men had a close relationship until it became clear in early 2006 that Rezko would be indicted on corruption charges.

In 1990, when Obama was making headlines at Harvard for becoming the first black president of the law review, Rezko offered him a job at Rezmar, his burgeoning low-income-housing firm. Obama declined the offer and took a job at Davis Miner instead. In 1995, Obama spent 32 hours, not five, working on a deal that enabled a non-profit run by his boss, Allison Davis, to join with Rezmar in acquiring an old nursing home and converting it into subsidized housing for poor people, according to the *Chicago Sun-Times*. That property—like many others Rezmar obtained using city, state, and federal loans—ended up in foreclosure at the taxpayers' expense.

In 1995, Obama also launched his first bid for the Illinois state senate, and Rezko was among his first contributors. Approximately $10,000 to $15,000 of the $100,000 that Obama hauled in during that campaign came from Rezko, according to an estimate Obama provided to the *Chicago Tribune*. Rezko continued to raise money for Obama during his subsequent state-senate races, his unsuccessful run for Congress in 2000, and his successful U.S. Senate run in 2004—about $250,000 in all.

Finally, when the Obamas were looking for a new house in the summer of 2005, Rezko helped them buy their dream home by purchasing an adjoining lot they could not afford, then selling them a strip of the land on which they wanted to build a fence. The real-estate deal attracted scrutiny after Rezko's indictment, and Obama has called it a "bone-headed move." But he told the *Tribune* that he did not see anything wrong with the deal at the time, because "I've known him for a long time. I assumed I would have seen a pattern [of corrupt behavior] over the past 15 years." Never mind that, by the summer of 2005, the Chicago papers had run over 100 stories about the clouds gathering over Rezko's head.

A month into the Rezko trial, it's just as hard to believe that Obama didn't see Rezko's pattern of corrupt behavior as it was to believe that he sat in Jeremiah Wright's pews for over 20 years and didn't see him damning America. In both cases, the more likely alternative is that he looked the other way. Rezko's whole business was the buying and selling of influence: It's how he became one of Chicago's biggest recipients of government loans to build low-income housing despite having no experience in real estate, and it's how—prosecutors allege—he built a corrupt network of political operatives to enrich himself and buy more influence.

Stuart Levine was one of these lower-level operatives. At Rezko's trial, he testified that he and Rezko conspired to use Levine's position on two state boards to benefit themselves and buy influence with Governor Blagojevich. In one such instance, Levine told the jury, he directed the Illinois Teachers Retirement System, of which he was a trustee, to invest $50 million with a firm called Glencoe Capital. In exchange, Levine arranged for himself and Rezko to split a fraudulent $500,000 "finder's fee." Rezko allegedly told Levine to route his half to an associate named Joseph Aramanda.

According to the indictment against Rezko, Aramanda "used the money . . . in substantial part for the benefit of Rezko." To that end, the indictment alleges, Aramanda received half of the money in March 2004 and wrote a $10,000 check to Barack Obama's Senate campaign that same month.

Of course, Obama has donated any and all Rezko-related contributions, including those he received from Aramanda, to charity, and he says neither he nor anyone on his campaign had any reason to suspect that Aramanda had obtained the money by fraudulent means.

Levine also offered testimony, backed up by wiretap evidence, which put Obama's former law-firm boss, Allison Davis, in the middle of an attempted quid pro quo. Davis's friend Thomas Rosenberg, a financier and the producer of the film *Million Dollar Baby*, was in line for a $220 million allocation from the Teachers Retirement System, but Levine was holding it up so that he and Rezko could attempt to extort money from Rosenberg.

Davis allegedly approached Rezko on Rosenberg's behalf and asked if a campaign contribution to Blagojevich would speed things along. Rezko told Davis to "call Stuart Levine." Rezko and Levine planned to give Rosenberg a choice: either pay a $2 million "finder's fee" or raise $1.5 million for Blagojevich.

When Rosenberg realized he was the target of such a massive shakedown, he was furious. In a recorded phone call that prosecutors played for the jury, one of Levine's co-schemers quoted Rosenberg's reaction: "'If [Tony Rezko and Blagojevich fundraiser Chris Kelly are] going to do this to me and think they're going to blackmail me, I'm going to take them down.'"

Rosenberg's threat convinced the alleged conspirators to back off, and—in the biggest bombshell to emerge during the trial so far—Levine testified that Rezko told him that Blagojevich had been informed of the situation and had agreed with Rezko's proposed course of action: to back off from the extortion plot but also to deny Rosenberg any more state contracts. Levine is not the most credible witness, but prosecutors played numerous recorded phone calls in which he discussed these schemes with co-conspirators in situations where it would have made little sense for him to lie.

If the allegations about Blagojevich are true, then such nakedly corrupt behavior at such a high level is bound to attract greater scrutiny from the national media on the problem of corruption in Illinois. Three out of the last seven elected Illinois governors have gone to jail for corruption, and based on evidence presented at the Rezko trial, Blagojevich could well become the fourth.

For Obama, this scrutiny would present a problem, not because he was involved in the serious wrongdoing for which Rezko is on trial, but because the evidence presented at his trial has made clear that Rezko's method of operating should have raised red flags for anyone doing business with him. Yet Obama did not distance himself from Rezko until the latter's indictment made him politically radioactive. We saw him do the same thing when the media discovered Jeremiah Wright's sermons. Obama wants us to believe he didn't really know his friends at all.

May 19, 2008

'Context,' You Say?

A guide to the radical theology of Rev. Jeremiah Wright

By Stanley Kurtz

What we've got here is failure to contextualize. If nothing else, Jeremiah Wright's defenders and enablers are right about that. To fully understand those "sound bites" and "snippets" calling on God to damn America, accusing the U.S. government of intentionally spreading HIV among blacks, and blaming 9/11 on America's allegedly terrorist history and foreign policy, we do need more context.

Far from exonerating Wright, however, removing those notorious sermon-segments from their endless video loop and firmly placing them in their social, political, historical, and theological context is even more damning (you'll forgive the expression) than the original YouTube videos. The full story of the Rev. Jeremiah Wright's theology and church adds considerable urgency to already-pressing questions about Barack Obama's judgment in choosing this man as his mentor and pastor.

Wright's defenders have portrayed Chicago's Trinity United Church of Christ as "well within the mainstream of the black church" while downplaying its militancy and politicization. In fact, Wright's church is not only thoroughly politicized, but is arguably the most radical black church in the country. The substance and style of Wright's infamous remarks are part and parcel of a broader, and proudly radical, theology. The bold denunciations are not distractions or somehow beside the point, but are the culmination and justification of Wright's prophetic vocation. Even his famous "Audacity to Hope" sermon, which led to Obama's conversion and baptism, fits into this framework.

A scarcely concealed, Marxist-inspired indictment of American capitalism pervades contemporary "black-liberation theology." Far from the mainstream, Trinity (and the relatively small band of other churches that share its worldview) sees itself as marginalized and radical, struggling in the face of an overwhelming rejection of its political theology by mainstream black churches.

THE FOUNDER

James H. Cone, founder and leading light of black-liberation theology, is the Charles A. Briggs Distinguished Professor of Systematic Theology at Union Theological Seminary, New York. Wright acknowledges Cone's work as the basis of Trinity's perspective, and Cone points to Trinity as the church that best exemplifies his message. Cone's 1969 book *Black Theology and Black Power* is the founding text of black-liberation theology, predating even much of the influential, Marxist-inspired liberation theology that swept Latin America in the 1970s. Cone's work is repeatedly echoed in Wright's sermons and statements. While Wright and Cone differ on some minor issues, Cone's theology is the first and best place to look for the intellectual context within which Wright's views took shape.

Cone credits Malcolm X—particularly his famous dismissal of Christianity as the white man's religion—with shaking him out of his theological complacency. In Malcolm's words:

> The white man has brainwashed us black people to fasten our gaze upon a blond-haired, blue-eyed Jesus! We're worshiping a Jesus that doesn't even *look* like us! Oh, yes! . . . The blond-haired, blue-eyed white man has taught you and me to worship a *white* Jesus, and to shout and sing and pray to this God that's *his* God, the white man's God. The white man has taught us to shout and sing and pray until we *die*, to wait until *death*, for some dreamy heaven-in-the-hereafter . . . while this white man has his milk and honey in the streets paved with golden dollars here on *this* earth!??

In the late 1960s, Malcolm X's criticisms (Wright calls them "devastating") were adopted by the founders of the black-power movement, such as Stokely Carmichael, the Black Panthers, and Ron Karenga. Shaken by Malcolm's rejection of Christianity and taken with the movement for black power, Cone, a young theologian and initially a devout follower of Martin Luther King Jr., set out to reconcile black power with Christianity. He did not reject Malcolm's disdain for a "blond-haired, blue-eyed Jesus"—rather, he came to believe that Jesus was black, and that an authentic Christianity, grounded in Jesus's blackness, would focus with full force on black liberation. Authentic Christianity would bring radical social and political transformation and, if necessary, violent revolution in the here and now.

Cone understood his task as both "radical" and "prophetic." It was radical in demanding deep transformation in the structure of society and prophetic in its determinedly angry and denunciatory tone. *Black Theology and Black Power*, says Cone in the book's introduction, is "written with a definite attitude, the attitude of an angry black man." Cone demands and commends anger, criticizes contemporary theologians for the "coolness" of their writings, and notes that "there is some evidence that Jesus got angry." In the book, Cone sometimes addresses or refers to whites as simply "the oppressor" or "Whitey."

The black intellectual's goal, says Cone, is to "aid in the destruction of America as he knows it." Such destruction requires both black anger and white guilt. The black-power theologian's goal is to tell the story of American oppression so powerfully and precisely that white men will "tremble, curse, and go mad, because they will be drenched with the filth of their evil." In the preface to his 1970 book, *A Black Theology of Liberation*, Wright wrote: "There will be no peace in America until whites begin to hate their whiteness, asking from the depths of their being: 'How can we become black?'"

So what exactly is "black power"? Echoing Malcolm X, Cone defines it as "complete emancipation of black people from white oppression by whatever means black people deem necessary." Open, violent rebellion is very much included in "whatever means"; like the radical anti-colonial theorist Frantz Fanon, on whom he sometimes draws, Cone sees violent rebellion as a transformative expression of the humanity of the oppressed. Drawing on existential theology, Cone defends those who looted during the urban riots of the late 1960s as affirming their "being," rather than simply grasping and destroying. Modifying Descartes, Cone explains the rioters' implicit message as "I rebel, therefore we exist."

LIBERAL RACISTS

While Cone asserts that blacks hate whites, he denies that this hatred is racism. Black racism, says Cone, is "a myth created by whites to ease their guilt feelings." Black hatred of whites is simply a legitimate reaction to "oppression, insult, and terror." Cone derides accusations of black racism as a mere "device of white liberals."

Indeed, one of the most striking features of *Black Theology and Black Power* is its strident attack on white liberals. According to Cone, "when white do-gooders are confronted with the style of Black Power, realizing that black people really place them in the same category with the George Wallaces, they react defensively, saying, 'It's not my fault' or 'I am not responsible.'" But Cone insists that white, liberal do-gooders are every bit as responsible as the most dyed-in-the-wool segregationists. Well before it became a cliché, Cone boldly set forth the argument for institutional racism—the notion that "racism is so embedded in the heart of American society that few, if any, whites can free themselves from it."

The liberal's favorite question, says Cone, is "What can I do?" He replies that, short of turning radical and putting their lives on the line behind a potentially violent revolution, liberals can do nothing. The real liberal question to blacks, says Cone, is "What can I do and still receive the same privileges as other whites *and*—this is the key—be liked by Negroes?" Again, he answers, "Nothing." To prove it, he pointedly dismisses the original bogus white liberal, Abraham Lincoln, who after all was more concerned with holding the Union together than with ending slavery.

For Cone, the deeply racist structure of American society leaves blacks with no alternative but radical transformation or social withdrawal. So-called Christianity, as commonly practiced in the United States, is actually the racist Antichrist. "Theologically," Cone affirms, "Malcolm X was not far wrong when he called the white man 'the devil.'" The false Christianity of the white-devil oppressor must be replaced by an authentic Christianity fully identified with the poor and oppressed:

> The religious ideas of the oppressor are detrimental to the
> black people's drive for freedom. They tend to make black peo-

ple non-violent and accept only the prescribed patterns of
protest defined by the oppressor himself. It is the oppressor
who attempts to tell black people what is and is not Christian—
though he is least qualified to make such a judgment.

To revolutionize or eliminate these faulty "white values," black pastors
and theologians must reject the influence of "white seminaries with their
middle-class white ideas about God, Christ, and the Church." "This does
not necessarily mean burning of their buildings with Molotov cocktails,"
says Cone. But it does require the replacement of middle-class consciousness with "black consciousness," with "a theology which *con-
fronts* white society as the racist Antichrist, communicating to the
oppressor that nothing will be spared in the fight for freedom."

So until the advent of a genuine revolution (in which, it is true, black
people would likely join with white radicals and poor whites against middle-class whites), blacks "must withdraw and form their own culture,
their own way of life." To regain their identity, they "must affirm the very
characteristic which the oppressor ridicules—*blackness*." Only such affir-
mation can counteract the deadly process in which black people have
been stripped of their culture and taught to hate their very blackness.

Cone's radicalism is evident in his categorical rejection of anything
short of total social revolution: "It does not matter how many gains are
made in civil rights. Progress is irrelevant." Black hatred of whites is
every bit as justified as hatred of Germans by Jews, says Cone. The
Jewish Holocaust was "one, big soul-wracking 'incident,'" but American
blacks endure a slow-motion holocaust in "constant jolts." For Cone,
then, short of revolution, white society cannot improve, and blacks are
enduring a perpetual de facto holocaust as long as they stay inside it.

STILL ANGRY

One might dismiss *Black Theology and Black Power* as a relic of the radical Sixties. As far as the vast majority of black churches are concerned,
that is true, but Trinity and a small group of radical congregations and
prestigious divinity schools don't see it that way. In those precincts,
Cone is lauded, and his early work is read, celebrated, and republished
in anniversary editions.

In 1998, in anticipation of the book's 30th anniversary, the

University of Chicago held a three-day conference in honor of *Black Theology and Black Power*. Martin Marty, the prominent University of Chicago historian of Christianity who once taught, and has lately defended, Wright, was a key sponsor of that conference. C-SPAN taped the event, and students (some of them still in high school), community members, and politicians (including Obama?) attended. Cone himself spoke, saying, "Thirty years later . . . I am still just as angry." Yet the most forceful testimony to the living power of Cone's text may be the fact that its outlines are reflected in nearly every aspect of the controversy surrounding Reverend Wright. Rumors of the Sixties' death, it would seem, are greatly exaggerated.

What exactly would Cone's ideal, post-revolutionary society look like? Cone has no better answer to that than did other Sixties revolutionaries, yet his fundamental social and economic perspective is Marxist. He would like to see capitalism replaced by some form of "democratic socialism." His nod to revolution in *Black Theology and Black Power* was not systematically Marxist, but after extended encounters with liberation theologians from Latin America in the 1970s, Cone took up Marx more seriously.

In his 1982 book, *My Soul Looks Back*, Cone updates us: "The black church cannot remain silent regarding socialism, because such silence will be interpreted by our Third World brothers and sisters as support for the capitalistic system, which exploits the poor all over this earth." And: "We cannot continue to speak against racism without any reference to a radical change in the economic order. I do not think that racism can be eliminated as long as capitalism remains intact."

But what about Marxism's rejection of God, and the claim that religion is the "opium of the people"? Cone concedes that white and black middle-class religion may stultify action, just as he conceded the soundness of Malcolm X's attack on dreamy, heaven-in-the-hereafter faith. Yet Cone argues that liberation theology is not an opiate but "a tonic that gives courage and strength in the struggle for freedom." The problem, says Cone, is not liberation theology but the false Christianity of middle-class blacks who are "upset with American society only because they want a larger piece of the capitalistic pie." Cone concludes: "Perhaps what we need today is to return to that 'good old-time religion' of our grandparents and combine with it a Marxist critique of society. Together black religion and Marxist philosophy may show us the way to build a completely new society."

Asked about these writings in a recent interview, Cone said, "I'm not a Marxist. . . . I'm a theologian, and I want to change society. I was searching for my way forward. I want a society in which people have the distribution of wealth, but I don't know quite how to do that institutionally." There is actually no contradiction between this carefully worded statement and Cone's position in *My Soul Looks Back*. He is chiefly a theologian, and has no specific economic program. Yet he seeks an alliance with Marxists and adopts a fundamentally Marxist analysis and critique of capitalism.

TRINITY TRANSFORMED

Cone's theology sheds revealing light on the history and social setting of Wright's early adulthood and later ministry at Trinity. In his first two years of college, Wright participated in the student civil-rights–sit-in movements of 1960 and 1961, where, he says, "I saw white Christian racism up close and 'in my face.'" While singing as a soloist in historically black Virginia Union University's traveling choir, Wright struggled to sort out his call to the ministry and his view of "the 'honkies' I was growing to hate with each passing day."

Years later, as Wright was completing a bachelor's degree at Howard University, also historically black, the school's famed choir sang only classical music. Gospel or jazz, and even more so African music, was forbidden. This did not sit well with Howard students, who rebelled during the turbulence that followed Martin Luther King's assassination in 1968 (just as Cone was composing *Black Theology and Black Power*). The Howard choir, with which Wright feels an ongoing connection, was outraged to be barred from singing Duke Ellington or Count Basie, even as these American geniuses were being granted honorary degrees by white schools. Says Wright, the choir was "tired of singing German lieder and Italian arias to prove they were intelligent. They wanted to sing their own music."

In those days, Trinity was one of the few predominantly black congregations in the liberal United Church of Christ denomination. Trinity had been formed by the UCC at the height of the early civil-rights movement, and the initial goal was to build a fully integrated church. Trinity's ethos was decidedly middle-class. "Unfortunately," says Wright, in those days "the notion of integration meant that blacks should adopt a white lifestyle, a white way of worship, European values, and European-American ways of viewing reality." Trinity's congregation sang hymns from "white hymnals," priding itself on services that could "out-white white people's services." In 1967, in a step viewed as misguided by today's Trinity congregants, the old Trinity rebuffed a call for cooperation from the Black Panther Party.

As the black-power movement spread in the wake of the King assassination, Trinity resisted. In the broader black community, post-'68, "aspirations for integration and assimilation were being replaced by those of black pride and separation," writes Julia Speller, a leader at today's Trinity, in her history of the congregation. While the old Trinity's middle-class congregants had enthusiastically supported the civil-rights movement, even this was challenged, says Speller, "as the African Americans of the nation lost faith in American systems and sought empowerment through self-help and revolution." Membership soon dwindled to 87 adults.

In 1972, Trinity finally decided to seek a more black-identified style of worship, and a fuller relationship with the surrounding black community. In Jeremiah Wright, with his raft of higher degrees and his desire to revive and develop black musical forms, Trinity believed it had found an ideal new pastor. Wright transformed Trinity's service—the choir took up quasi-dance stepping and swaying moves, along with African dashikis, drums, tambourines, and washboards—and the congregation grew exponentially.

Although Trinity had brought on Wright with change in mind, the original congregants were not prepared for the extremes to which Wright's "Africentrism" and black-liberation theology would take him. Wright arrived in 1972, and by 1975 nearly all of the members who had originally invited him had left. In 1983 a group of particularly active and prominent members uncomfortable with Wright left Trinity and the UCC for a local Pentecostal Apostolic church.

In 1978 there was trouble with the UCC as well, as a national-level official attempted to distance the church from Trinity. Says Speller,

"Trinity was accused of being a cult (only three months after Jim Jones and Jonestown!) and Wright of having an 'ego problem.'" The unnamed official failed in his efforts, and after church-sponsored attempts at "reconciliation" offered an apology to Trinity.

INTO AFRICA

Although Wright had been nominally Africentric all along, it was not until the late 1980s that he actually traveled to Africa. These visits provoked a change in his thinking. In *Black Theology and Black Power*, Cone had spoken as if blacks had been essentially stripped of their African heritage by slavery. Wright had never been fully comfortable with this view, and instead had stressed continuities between Africans and American blacks. Now, after seeing Africa, Wright moved seriously in the direction of identification with Africa, infusing his sermons and worship at Trinity with anti-apartheid (and other Africa-related) political activism. This, of course, was the very moment at which Barack Obama, still trying to reconcile his own complex African and American identities, encountered Wright.

The 1988 "Audacity to Hope" sermon invoked the privation and oppression of "black and brown" citizens in Africa and the rest of the world. To a superficial ear, the sermon may seem simply to call for aid to the world's hungry. For those attuned to Wright's theology, however, it contains a scarcely veiled attack on Western capitalism, which Wright believes is the true cause of the suffering and privation of the "black and brown" world.

There are several different transcripts of the "Audacity" speech—Wright gave it multiple times, changing it along the way, and some published versions may be toned down for general consumption. But the one included in *What Makes You So Strong?*, a collection of Wright speeches, attacks "white America's corporate dollars that hold and pull the purse strings of so many national black organizations." For Wright, this corporate money turns middle-class blacks into "slaves."

So Wright believes that American capitalism is both the underlying cause of the poverty and suffering of black people abroad, and the sinfully tempting apple that lures deluded middle-class blacks to enslave themselves to corporate white America. In this he follows Cone. Attacks on capitalism are scattered throughout Wright's sermons, and it is difficult to believe that someone as sharp as Obama could have failed to pick up on this radical message. Indeed, it's difficult to read or hear almost anything by Wright without figuring it out.

Wright's Cone connection remains strong. Cone's recent work argues that the crucifixion of Jesus was essentially a public lynching, with the Romans anticipating the role of modern white Americans. This analogy shapes the recent sermon/article in which Wright refers to ancient Roman "garlic noses." Wright's invocation of Thomas Jefferson's "pedophilia" (i.e., Jefferson's relationship with Sally Hemings) also echoes recent remarks by Cone.

Sadly, the excesses of "middle-class black assimilationism"—such as denying choirs access to greats like Duke Ellington and Count Basie—provoked in Cone and Wright a still more extreme and damaging counter-response. The tragedy is that the members of the old Trinity seem to have genuinely sought a middle way. They were ready for a shift away from assimilationist extremes, yet they refused to repudiate "middle-classness" or embrace a radical rejection of American culture.

Wright, Cone, and the academics and politicians who excuse and enable them are stuck in a late-Sixties time warp. To Wright, middle-class blacks are abandoning poor blacks to gain a piece of the capitalist pie. The tragedy of the 1990s, says Wright, is that "most African Americans have now given psychological assent to their oppressors and to their enslavement. We have gotten the chains off our bodies and put them on our minds!"

FALSE ANALOGIES

Defenders of Trinity's Africentrism compare it to the harmless Celticentrism of Catholic churches that are predominately Irish. This analogy is flawed—such churches do not insist that Jesus was Irish, that his ministry was identified solely with the sufferings of the Irish oppressed, that non-Irish churches are the Antichrist, or that middle-class Irish who foolishly ape mainstream American ways are collaborating in their own enslavement to an intrinsically oppressive capitalist system. If Irish Catholics had been Celticentric in this sense, the great success story of Irish-immigrant assimilation would never have been written. And had

Wright expanded the elements of black culture at Trinity without actually repudiating black aspirations to fully join the American middle class, as the original congregants had hoped, it might have opened up a far better solution for Chicago's blacks. That road not taken would have been the real analogue to the Celticentrism of Irish Catholic churches.

At the heart of Cone's and Wright's refusals to enter the mainstream of American culture lies the ongoing conviction that, appearances to the contrary, nothing in American race relations has improved. No matter how different things look today, it's all just a disguised form of slavery or holocaust. Cone's original attempt to justify black hatred of whites by equating America with Nazi Germany was unconvincing, but the slavery/Holocaust analogy lives on as the indispensable linchpin of black-liberation theology.

Ultimately, this theological need to see slavery and holocaust alive in the American present (along with Cone's call for angry, prophetic denunciations) stands behind Wright's infamous sermon clips. In 2005, Wright co-edited an anthology of essays called *Blow the Trumpet in Zion*. In that reader, Cone singles out the large black prison population as the latest example of "the nearly four-hundred-year-long history of terror against Black people in the United States." Of course, this same theme appears in Wright's notorious "sound bites" and "snippets." Wright embraces the canard that the U.S. government is intentionally infecting the black population with HIV to justify his theological notion of an ongoing holocaust—and thereby validate his refusal to make peace with America or its capitalist system. Echoing Cone's early writings, another essay from *Blow the Trumpet in Zion* castigates preachers for being "so mealymouthed" when it comes to denouncing political evil. Obviously, Wright has taken that message to heart.

Wright's denunciation of America for bringing 9/11 on itself explicitly invokes Malcolm X's notorious claim that John F. Kennedy's assassination was a case of America's chickens coming home to roost. Wright's tale of America's long history of "terrorism"—from our attacks on the Indians, to our attacks on Cubans in Grenada (Wright has visited Cuba three times), to our bombing of Muammar Qaddafi, to America's support for Israel's "state terrorism"—comes straight out of Cone's historical playbook.

More deeply, Wright's view of 9/11 parallels Cone's startling attacks on "liberal do-gooders." Cone refuses to concede that white liberals can be innocent of racism. In the same fashion, Wright refuses to concede American innocence in the matter of 9/11. Since Wright sees American capitalism and the military power that defends it as fundamentally responsible for the world's misery, no American can escape guilt for his participation in this system.

CONTEXT

When we consider that nearly the whole of Wright's original congregation left, that other active members departed, and that Wright's radicalism made relations in the United Church of Christ rocky, Barack Obama's decision to stay appears all the more striking. Indeed, *Blow the Trumpet in Zion* is filled with attempts by Cone's followers to come to grips with their rejection by the broader black community. Nearly every sermon Wright preaches, as well as his now-infamous bulletins and church magazines, is filled with his radicalism, and it's therefore impossible not to conclude that Obama was broadly attracted to Wright's politics. Interestingly, Obama's remarks on unemployed workers' clinging to conventional religion as a sop are not at all inconsistent with Cone's or Wright's—or for that matter Malcolm X's—views.

Obama has now attempted to distance himself from Wright, claiming to be "outraged" by the reverend's recent comments. Yet it's hard to believe that Obama heard anything in the past few weeks that he hadn't heard before. What gives outrage only now has been going on for decades.

In his rejection of the path of assimilation; in his contempt for "middle-classness" and the capitalist system it sustains; in his pursuit of a separate, black Christianity and his hostility to conventional religion; in his bitter and "prophetic" denunciations of America's history, its founding icons and its anti-Qaddafi, pro-Israel foreign policy; in his conviction that the U.S. government is responsible for genocide against blacks; and in his insistence that Americans are collectively guilty for 9/11, Jeremiah Wright is a true follower of James Cone's theology of black liberation. It would seem the only thing worse than quoting Jeremiah Wright out of context is quoting him in context.

November 3, 2008

The Real Ayers Issue

It's about revolution, not terrorism

By Andrew C. McCarthy

"*L a educación es revolución!*" Bill Ayers, the former Weatherman terrorist who is Barack Obama's friend and "education reform" collaborator, was opening the World Education Forum in Venezuela. It was just two years ago, November 2006. As a beaming Hugo Chávez looked on, Ayers roused a throng of "invited guests, comrades," touting the world's classrooms as the front-line for the Left's anti-American revolution.

Ayers has never made a secret of the fact that he is not just a man of the Left but a *revolutionary*. The revolution in the classroom, he repeat-edly and defiantly maintains, is the same revolution he has served for 40 years, the same revolution that inspired him to bomb the Pentagon, the U.S. Capitol, and other American targets beginning in the late Sixties. On this day in Caracas, he gushed with praise for Chávez's "Bolivarian Revolution and . . . the profound educational reforms underway here in Venezuela." Against capitalism—which, he said, "promotes racism and materialism" and "turn[s] people into consumers, not citizens"—he con-trasted Chávez's police state: a "beacon to the world."

In the electoral stretch-run, as concerns mount over his long associ-ation with Ayers, Barack Obama and his campaign have finally settled on a curt narrative: Obama was only eight years old when Ayers carried out "detestable" terrorist bombings. As critics of the Ayers tie append "unrepentant terrorist" to each mention of Ayers's name, Obama parti-sans deftly deflect the outrage: "So what are you saying, that Obama is a terrorist?"

No one is actually saying that, so the critics are duly cowed. As they shrink from the bracing linkage of *Obama* and *terrorist*, the relieved Obamedia brush the entirety of their case aside.

Of course, Ayers's terrorism is relevant. Americans are right to wonder why Obama would consort with such an execrable figure. But it has never been the main issue. When it comes to Ayers, it's revolutionary Leftism that matters. The ideology that drives Ayers is what drew Obama to him.

Discomfited by the increased scrutiny over Ayers, Obama counters with elite academia's imprimatur: Ayers is now a distinguished education professor at the University of Illinois at Chicago. Just last March, the 25,000-member American Educational Research Association elected Ayers its vice president for curriculum. These attainments, though, are no answer. Americans are inured to the non-stop excesses of what Roger Kimball calls our "tenured radicals." Accolades from the academy do little to assuage concerns about Obama's dalliance with a bomber whose only regret is his failure to have carried out more bombings.

And would that it were just a dalliance! Obama's dishonesty about the relationship has slowly become obvious. First, he tried to minimize Ayers as just "a guy who lives in my neighborhood." Obama's campaign risibly told the credulous *New York Times* that he and the former terrorist met for the first time in late 1995 at the Ayers home, where Ayers and his wife, former Weather Underground terrorist Bernardine Dohrn, hosted the event that launched Obama's political career.

Inevitably, thanks largely to the dogged research of *National Review*'s Stanley Kurtz, it emerged that Obama and Ayers had collaborated on a six-year, $160 million "education reform" project known as the Chicago Annenberg Challenge. The CAC was the brainchild of Ayers, who ran its operational arm. Obama was brought in to chair the board that approved program grants: tens of millions of dollars that seeded such leftist redoubts as the Small Schools Workshop—run by Mike Klonsky, Ayers's Maoist associate—and ACORN (the Association of Community Organizations for Reform Now), a group (long associated with Obama) whose fraudulent voter-registration practices are now tainting yet another election cycle.

Obama and his allies have shifted their version of events as new facts have trickled out. In October, the *Times*—in an attempt to whitewash the Ayers tie—tacitly revised its prior reporting (which had neglected to mention the little matter of the CAC, the candidate's only significant executive experience). The first encounter between Obama and Ayers was now supposed to have been "a lunchtime meeting about school reform in a Chicago skyscraper" some months before Obama's famous debut in the Ayers living room. This, too, is implausible. At the time, Obama was an unknown, inexperienced, 33-year-old third-year associate at a small Chicago law firm. Would a committed activist like Ayers, whose allies had been hardcore radicals willing to die for the cause, entrust the goldmine that would bankroll his revolution to such a novice just because Obama made a nice impression over salad?

The origins of the relationship remain shrouded in mystery, though clues abound. Obama and Ayers walked the same path from Morningside Heights to Hyde Park. Obama was a student at Columbia from 1981 to 1983. He refuses to discuss those years; it is known only that he studied for at least some time under Edward Said, the late PLO apologist. Ayers first settled near Columbia when he and Dohrn emerged from fugitivity in 1980. Perhaps coincidentally (and perhaps not), Ayers is an ardent admirer of Said, who (like Obama) heaped glowing public praise on one of Ayers's books. And years later, when they sat together on the board of the left-leaning Woods Fund in Chicago, Obama and Ayers financially supported Rashid Khalidi, another Arafat devotee who left the University of Chicago to become Columbia's Edward Said Professor of Middle East Studies.

While Obama was at Columbia, Ayers studied at nearby Bank Street College of Education. After graduating from Columbia, Obama soon became a "community organizer" in Harlem before relocating to Chicago in 1985 to direct the Developing Communities Project (an off-shoot of the Gamaliel Foundation, dedicated to Saul Alinsky's principles for radicalizing society). Ayers, meanwhile, remained in the Harlem area until 1987, when he received his doctorate at Columbia's Teachers College and went off to teach at UIC.

In Chicago, both men became embroiled in a major education controversy that resulted in citywide reform legislation in 1988. By then, though she could not be admitted to the bar due to a prior contempt citation, Bernardine Dohrn was working at Chicago's prestigious Sidley Austin law firm, an intern position she secured with the help of Ayers's father, the influential Chicago businessman Tom Ayers—a staunch liberal who was also enmeshed in the education-reform effort. At Sidley, Dohrn overlapped with Obama's wife, Michelle, then an associate at the firm. Dohrn left Sidley in 1988, shortly before Obama arrived there as a summer intern after his first year at Harvard Law School.

Now, maybe it's true that a pair of guys who, beginning in 1981, traveled the same path, admired some of the same people, drifted through Chicago's leftist circles, and embraced the same "reform" cause really didn't know each other until they became fast friends and partners in 1995. Pardon my skepticism. There is, in any event, enough common ground here that Obama, having failed to make Ayers disappear, is now trying to marginalize him—preposterously. So we have David Axelrod, Obama's top political adviser, hilariously chirping, "*There's no evidence that they're close.*" (Emphasis added.) Translation: Get back to us when you have more damaging information—until then, we don't need to refine our story further.

Yet they do refine away, as the evidence mounts. Obama first grudgingly admitted that Ayers wasn't just "a guy who lives in my neighborhood," but a guy with whom he sat on a couple of boards and with whom he occasionally sat on panels. Yet even this new account is impossible to square with the lengthy partnership, the dollars involved, and the fact that at least one of their joint panel appearances (at the University of Chicago) was arranged by Michelle Obama, then an associate dean—to say nothing of the rave review ("a searing and timely account") Obama wrote in 1997 for *A Kind and Just Parent*, Ayers's leftist polemic against the criminal justice system.

So Obama tried yet another tack: He didn't know about Ayers's terrorist past when they first became associated in 1995. But that won't fly either. Ayers is proud of his past. For a leftist revolutionary, constructed history is a tool of the trade, so sure, Ayers falsely claims the Weathermen took pains to do only property damage, not kill or maim people. Besides that, though, he can't stop talking about, and urging others to draw lessons from, his bomber days. (I'll leave aside that he and Dohrn raised a child of their co-conspirators, who are serving lengthy sentences for the Brinks murders, and named one of their sons after a Black Panther killed in a shootout in which a New Jersey state trooper was murdered.)

Obama—intelligent, highly educated, and (as he has written) extremely careful about his associations—unquestionably knew exactly who Ayers was. And in the inconceivable event that he didn't, he would no doubt have learned about it from Ayers in the first five minutes.

So now we're on to Version Three (or thereabouts): Obama *might possibly* have known who Ayers was, but he thought Ayers had been "rehabilitated" as a nationally renowned educator. Ayers, however, has never been a mere educator. He is, by his own account, a leftist revolutionary, an activist who sees the classroom as a more promising battlefield—or, as he puts it, "contested space"—than the Pentagon or the Capitol.

"Do you really think Obama is a terrorist?" No. It wasn't Ayers's terrorism that attracted Obama. It was Ayers's leftist revolution. We can take Obama at his word that he condemns the bombings. But Obama was front and center for the revolution.

Ayers's revolution is Obama's "change." Ayers's "participatory democracy" through "popular empowerment" is Obama's ACORN. Ayers's rage against the criminal justice system that paints America as an apartheid state and prison as a fading antique is Obama's "searing and timely account." The joint Ayers/Obama pursuit of "social justice" is seen in their joint underwriting (through the Woods Fund) of Marxist black-liberation theology at Jeremiah Wright's Trinity Church, and of Khalidi's Arab American Action Network—an organization that condones Palestinian terror while promoting public welfare and drivers' licenses for illegal aliens in the U.S. Further, when it comes to "education reform," the most significant of the duo's shared passions, capitalism is the root cause of racism while Chávez's Venezuela is "a beacon to the world."

Obama may have been eight years old when Ayers bombed the Pentagon. But he was Ayers's partner in 1995 when the former terrorist was publicly describing himself as "a radical, leftist, small-'c' communist." Obama was an elected official in Illinois when, on 9/11, the *Times* published Ayers's sentiments that he regretted only failing to set more bombs and (a few days later) that America still "makes me want to puke." Obama was a U.S. senator planning a presidential run in 2006 when Ayers made his speech in Caracas—and when he gave an interview to *Revolution* magazine (the self-styled "Voice of the Revolutionary Communist Party, USA") in which he decried the plight of Ward Churchill (the radical former University of Colorado professor who called 9/11 victims "little Eichmanns"): "How can we as socialists or as communists or as leftists, how can we leave him in the cold?"

Ayers is Ayers, has always been, and doesn't pretend to be anything else. And Obama chose to be his friend and collaborator.

November 3, 2008

Barack's Grenade-Lobber

Meet political strategist David Axelrod

By Mark Hemingway

I magine the following scenario: A handsome, charismatic minority candidate defeats a heavily favored Democratic insider for the presidential nomination in an acrimonious race that drags out all the way to the convention. He then finds himself running in the general election against an aging, moderate Republican senator frequently at odds with his own party.

The current presidential race? Maybe, but it's also the plot of the final season of *The West Wing*, which aired in 2005 and 2006. The similarities are not entirely coincidental.

Barack Obama's chief strategist, legendary political consultant David Axelrod, was fresh off Obama's successful Senate race when Eli Attie, a former speechwriter to Al Gore who was writing for *The West Wing*, had several conversations with him. Attie says he drew considerable inspiration from Axelrod's impressions of Obama when conjuring Hispanic congressman Matt Santos, the successful dark-horse candidate on the show. Earlier this year, the web magazine *Slate* even edited the speeches of Obama and Santos together into an almost indistinguishable whole.

It appears that Axelrod, after decades of tinkering in the political laboratory, finally has in Barack Obama the perfect embodiment of his ideas about what makes a candidate appealing. Sometimes it's hard to know where Axelrod ends and Obama begins—a lengthy profile of Axelrod in *The New York Times Magazine* observed: "When he talks about his own ideas, Axelrod has a habit of substituting anecdotes not from his own life but from Obama's . . . as if his is a compounded, and cultivated, existence." Indeed, a close look at the career of David Axelrod suggests that Obama is the magnum opus of a brilliant political consultant.

Axelrod was raised in New York, the son of a psychologist father and a mother who worked for the left-wing newspaper PM in the 1940s. (David Mendell's *Obama: From Promise to Power* quotes Axelrod's referring to his parents as "classic New York leftists.") Axelrod began working as a journalist while still an undergrad at the University of Chicago, and was hired by the *Chicago Tribune* straight out of college. The paper soon let him loose on City Hall, but Axelrod wasn't content to sit on the sidelines, and many believe he used his perch to champion the 1979 mayoral candidacy of Jane Byrne. Against the odds Byrne got elected, but her mayoralty was not successful, and Axelrod's coverage turned accordingly negative.

Axelrod left the paper in 1984, citing (according to Mendell) concerns over its "corporatization" and disagreements with his superiors. When Axelrod walked away from the *Tribune*, he was unusually close to Chicago's influential media players and labyrinthine political establishment. Despite having no real political experience, he was almost immediately hired by Democrat Paul Simon. Axelrod helped handle Simon's ultimately successful Senate bid, and the consultant's career took off like a rocket. Of the eight candidates who ran for the Democratic presidential nomination this election, Axelrod had worked for five.

Axelrod is known for two things. One is race. He has been particularly adept at running black candidates and helping them win support from white voters. He has helped elect black mayors in Cleveland and Chicago, as well as in majority-black cities such as Detroit and Washington, D.C. In 2006 he helped elect Deval Patrick, the current governor of Massachusetts and the first black person to hold that office. Patrick's election was seen by many as a trial run for Obama's presidential campaign. The themes are notably similar. Patrick's slogan was "Together We Can." And, as Hillary Clinton's campaign noted at the time, one of Obama's speeches heavily plagiarized one of Patrick's. Axelrod was probably the primary author of both.

The second thing that distinguishes Axelrod is his willingness to be merciless, even borderline underhanded, to political opponents. Republican consultants fear him. Ed Rollins, who's handled campaigns ranging from Ronald Reagan's 1984 presidential bid to Mike Huckabee's shot at the nomination this year, put Axelrod on the top of his list of "guys I never want to see lobbing grenades at me again." Mike Murphy, who's advised Arnold Schwarzenegger and Mitt Romney, calls Axelrod "very, very dangerous."

Before Axelrod signed on with Obama's Senate campaign, he interviewed to work for Blair Hull—Obama's main challenger and then the favorite to win the Democratic primary. A former professional gambler turned securities trader, Hull was exceedingly wealthy and willing to spend millions. During interviews with Hull, Axelrod mentioned some ugly rumors surrounding Hull's divorce. Hull acknowledged the rumors but declined to give Axelrod specifics. Axelrod eventually joined Obama's Senate campaign and, wouldn't you know it, right as Obama's television ads began in earnest, the details of Hull's divorce surfaced in the *Tribune*. Many found the timing suspicious—even if Axelrod wasn't given details, he had a good idea of Hull's vulnerabilities and where to start looking for the dirt.

Axelrod is an expert at clandestine political attacks. According to *BusinessWeek*, he is the "master of 'Astroturfing'"—the art of planting messages on the Internet and elsewhere to make it look like there's a grassroots movement supporting your position. Axelrod operates ASK Public Strategies, an incredibly secretive PR company that "discreetly plots strategy and advertising campaigns for corporate clients to tilt public opinion their way." Axelrod won't talk about ASK and has rebuffed media requests to see a client list, though *BusinessWeek* determined the firm had worked for big-name corporate clients such as AT&T and Cablevision.

Throughout the presidential campaign a number of suspicious "anonymous" attacks have been traced back to the Obama camp. First, an anti-Hillary YouTube video (parodying Apple's infamous 1984 Super Bowl ad) turned into an Internet sensation, with 2 million views in two weeks. Obama's campaign denied involvement, but it was later revealed that the ad's creator had multiple ties to the campaign, and had lived with the campaign's press secretary. More recently, a professional PR firm with extensive Democratic ties was caught uploading videos to YouTube that spread falsehoods about Sarah Palin. The videos used the same voiceover artist employed by Axelrod's firm and the Obama campaign. Similar incidents abound.

If there's any common thread to Axelrod's work in politics, it's that—as *The Economist* recently put it—he "firmly believes that the candidate is the message. The important thing is to tell a positive story about the candidate rather than to muddy the narrative with lots of talk about policy details." Unlike many political consultants, Axelrod is not known for his interest in policy; his acumen appears to stop at the water's edge of governance. He is drawn to candidates who are exciting, rather than proven or capable.

Many of the politicians he has supported, starting with Byrne, have failed in office. Patrick's governorship has been unpopular, marked by fiascos involving the gutting of educational standards and a failed attempt to expand gambling in Massachusetts to deal with overwhelming budget woes. And the administration of Chicago mayor Richard M. Daley—whom Axelrod faithfully supports—has been marked by rampant corruption. Former Chicago alderman and University of Illinois political science professor Dick Simpson told the *New York Times*, "David Axelrod's mostly been visible in Chicago in the last decade as Daley's public relations strategist and the guy who goes on television to defend Daley from charges of corruption."

For the inexperienced Obama, a better comparison than *The West Wing* might be Robert Redford's *Candidate*, in which some shrewd political consultants help an inexperienced lawyer run for office. Having won the race, all Redford's character can do is stare and ask, "Now what?" Should Obama ask that question, it's unlikely Axelrod will have answers.

March 9, 2009

Lawyer's Lawyer, Radical's Radical

Meet Obama DOJ nominee Dawn Johnsen

By Andrew C. McCarthy

Pregnancy provokes a welter of feelings, physical and emotional. But does anyone really think of pregnancy as slavery? Apparently so: Indiana University law professor Dawn Johnsen, Pres. Barack Obama's nominee to head the Justice Department's Office of Legal Counsel.

Yale-educated and ACLU-trained, Johnsen already has done one tour of duty at OLC. She spent nearly six years there during the Clinton administration (1993–98), the last two as acting chief. OLC, a critically important agency, is the administration's lawyers' lawyer. Staffed by graduates of top law schools who are then polished by elite judicial clerkships, it authoritatively interprets the law for the attorney general and, in doing so, drives administration legal policy. OLC's credibility is derived from its reputation for apolitical, academic discipline—its commitment to informing policymakers of what the law is, rather than what staffers believe the law should be. Johnsen is, for that reason, a poor fit: She is an ideologue, and an unabashed one.

Her bizarre equation of pregnancy and slavery was not an off-the-cuff remark. It was her considered position in a 1989 brief filed in the Supreme Court. At the time, she was legal director of NARAL (then the National Abortion Rights Action League, since renamed NARAL Pro-Choice America). The case, *Webster v. Reproductive Health Services*, involved a Missouri law that did not ban abortion but restricted the use of state funds and resources for abortions. It's an obvious distinction, but one without a difference—at least according to Johnsen. Any restriction that makes abortion less accessible is, in her view, tantamount to "involuntary servitude" because it "requires a woman to provide continuous physical service to the fetus in order to further the state's asserted interest [in the life of the unborn]." In effect, a woman "is constantly aware for nine months that her body is not her own: the state has conscripted her body for its own ends." Such "forced pregnancy," she contends, violates the Thirteenth Amendment, which prohibits slavery.

The Court rejected this farcical theory, just as it has rejected other instantiations of Johnsen's extremism. On abortion and other issues dear to the Left, she is nothing short of a zealot. She insisted that, without government-provided abortion counseling, a large number of women would be left without "proper information about contraception." This, she claimed, would mean they "cannot be said to have a meaningful opportunity to avoid pregnancy." The usual rejoinder to such reasoning is that nobody is forcing these women to have sex. Johnsen sees it differently, writing that these "losers in the contraceptive lottery no more 'consent' to pregnancy than pedestrians 'consent' to being struck by drunk drivers."

In reputable private law offices and U.S. attorney's offices throughout the country, adult supervision would prevent such a lunatic analogy from finding its way into a letter to a lower-court judge, much less into a Supreme Court brief. Obama, however, is proposing that Johnsen be the adult supervision at Justice. He would fill a position calling for dispassionate rigor with a crusader for whom strident excess is habitual.

For Johnsen, no impediment to abortion-on-demand passes muster: She opposes 24-hour waiting periods, parental-consent requirements for minors, and laws against partial-birth abortion. In 2007, when it upheld the partial-birth ban in *Gonzales v. Carhart*, the Supreme Court clinically described the standard abortion procedure (i.e., the dismemberment and evacuation of the unborn child) to contrast it with the more barbaric partial-birth method. Johnsen's reaction—voiced while proposing "A Progressive Agenda for Women's Reproductive Health and Liberty" for the left-leaning American Constitution Society—was to complain that "every first-year law student's constitutional law casebook" now contains "gruesome descriptions designed to make abortions sound like infanticide." Moreover, as she declaimed in a 2006 op-ed opposing Samuel Alito's confirmation, opposition to all restrictions on abortion— not just acceptance of *Roe v. Wade*—should be a litmus test for judicial nominees. "The notion of legal restrictions as some kind of reasonable 'compromise'—perhaps to help make abortion 'safe, legal, and rare,'" she wrote, "proves nonsensical."

Johnsen's other *bête noire* is national security—at least to the extent it involves detaining terrorists and enemy combatants as military opponents rather trying them as civilian criminal defendants. Her 2008 academic article "What's a President to Do? Interpreting the Constitution in the Wake of Bush Administration Abuses" gathers the Left's full array of anti-war tropes and disguises them as legal analysis. There is the determination to ignore the terrorist attacks of the 1990s, such that the War on Terror is presented as something President Bush started after 9/11 rather than a years-long jihadist provocation to which the United States finally responded after 9/11. This framework would make it impossible to prosecute as war crimes such pre-9/11 atrocities as the bombings of the USS *Cole* and the embassies in East Africa. Johnsen further denigrates as an "extreme and implausible Commander-in-Chief theory" Bush's rationale for warrantless surveillance of suspected al-Qaeda communications into and out of the United States. In fact, the practice was strongly supported by federal court precedent and has since been reaffirmed by the appellate court Congress created specifically to consider such issues. And Johnsen has recently written that the new administration "should order an immediate review to determine which detainees should be released and which transferred to secure facilities in the United States" for civilian trials.

It is especially galling to consider Johnsen's smearing of John Yoo, the Cal-Berkeley law professor who, as a Bush OLC staffer, principally authored DOJ's so-called torture memo. In contrast to Johnsen's perversion of anti-slavery law to suit her abortion agenda, Yoo was not twisting the law to advocate torture. He was soberly attempting to construe a legal term, "severe . . . pain or suffering," part of the statutory definition of torture that had not yet been interpreted by the courts. This is what OLC does: It struggles to understand the state of the law, irrespective of staffers' predilections, so that policymakers can act in full awareness of their options. For this, Johnsen impugns not merely Yoo's scholarship ("irresponsibly and dangerously false") but also his good faith. She upbraids the Bush administration for its use of waterboarding to interrogate top al-Qaeda detainees, blithely presuming its illegality despite the complex questions surrounding that claim (including the fact that that Congress has declined to make waterboarding a war crime). Indifferent to the fact that our enemies train to resist known interrogation methods, Johnsen wants all tactics spelled out explicitly in advance.

Particularly rich is Johnsen's diatribe against Bush's purportedly outlandish claim of power to ignore statutes that encroach on executive authority. When Johnsen served in the Clinton administration (which invented extraordinary rendition, detained Cuban refugees without trial at Guantanamo Bay, conducted warrantless national-security searches, and attacked a foreign country without congressional authorization), OLC's official position was that "the President has enhanced responsibility to resist unconstitutional provisions that encroach upon the constitutional powers of the Presidency." The office opined that several statutes (including privacy provisions in the federal wiretap law) could not bind the president, and Johnsen herself authored a 1997 OLC opinion concluding that presidents were above consumer-credit-disclosure laws. In that case, she broadly asserted that "statutes that do not expressly apply to the President must be construed as not applying to him if such application would involve a possible conflict with his constitutional prerogatives."

A parallel hypocrisy is illustrated by Johnsen's rants about how the Bush administration "politicized" the Justice Department. Her solution to this problem: Politicize the Justice Department. She argues that job applicants who may have been passed over by the Bush administration for holding leftist political views should get "special consideration" in DOJ hiring but, at the same time, maintains that nominees for the federal judiciary should be rejected out of hand if they embrace constitutional originalism or are members of the judicially conservative Federalist Society. Johnsen would also press the DOJ to advance the leftist agenda by having its Environment and Natural Resource Division "pursue innovative litigation and policy initiatives, such as the pressing issue of climate change."

Johnsen's attraction for Obama is obvious. The principal target of her *Webster* brief was the settled principle that the Constitution's recognition of various fundamental rights (and the judicial invention of such "rights" as abortion) does not confer an entitlement to governmental aid to exercise those rights. For Johnsen, this is anathema, the denial of "economic justice" and thus of equal protection. "Economic justice," a favorite Obama phrase, is the Left's euphemism for the "redistributive change" Obama criticized the radical Warren Court for failing to embrace. Rather than the hoary construction of the Constitution as "a charter of negative liberties," one that says only what government "can't do to you," Obama urges a new bill of rights defining what government "must do on your behalf."

In Dawn Johnsen's dizzying jurisprudence, government has no business invading individual privacy and regulating abortion but is obliged to coerce taxpayers into underwriting abortions as a first step in what she unapologetically calls "the progressive agenda" of "universal health care, public funding for childcare, paid family leave, and . . . the full range of economic justice issues, from the minimum wage to taxation policy to financial support for struggling families."

If Johnsen is confirmed, OLC will be transformed from a source of non-ideological legal analysis to a culture-war agitator. And its value to the Department of Justice may be lost.

November 2, 2009

Every-Which-Way Joe

The Vice President's plan for Afghanistan is only his latest exercise in folly and self-contradiction

By Jamie M. Fly

Writing in the July/August 2007 issue of *Foreign Affairs*, then-candidate Barack Obama outlined his foreign-policy views. He wrote that after the financial and human cost of the Iraq War, "many Americans may be tempted to turn inward and cede our leadership in world affairs. But this is a mistake we must not make. America cannot meet the threats of this century alone, and the world cannot meet them without America."

He then harkened back to three Democratic presidents:

> Such leadership demands that we retrieve a fundamental insight of Roosevelt, Truman, and Kennedy—one that is truer now than ever before: the security and well-being of each and every American depend on the security and well-being of those who live beyond our borders.

This statement may seem somewhat surprising given that Democrats spent much of the Bush presidency questioning President Bush's interventions abroad, and that even as Senator Obama wrote these words he and many in his party were advocating the abandonment of the Iraqi people to sectarian bloodshed.

Democratic foreign policy since the end of the Cold War has been characterized by this dichotomy between U.S. international engagement and a more restrictive view of America's international obligations. A majority of Democratic senators voted against the 1991 Persian Gulf War. The Clinton administration intervened in Bosnia, Haiti, and

Kosovo, repeatedly bombed Iraq, and went after Osama bin Laden with cruise missiles. In the wake of the September 11 attacks, a majority of Democratic senators supported the Iraq War, but the Left turned against the war and today is lobbying President Obama to pull out of Afghanistan.

This Democratic uncertainty about America's role in the world and its ability to effect change overseas is apparent once again as President Obama's national-security team discusses the way ahead in Afghanistan. Gen. Stanley McChrystal has submitted an assessment stating that, without additional forces, the U.S. effort in Afghanistan "will likely result in failure."

The chief opponent of General McChrystal and the military brass is an unlikely one: Vice President Joe Biden. Unlikely because for much of the last eight years, Biden criticized Vice President Cheney for his supposedly oversized role in policymaking, especially on national-security issues.

Earlier this year, Biden lost the first round when President Obama rejected his advice and decided to send 4,000 troops to Afghanistan beyond the 17,000 he had already authorized, but the vice president has now resumed his advocacy for a "counterterrorism" approach. This approach would narrow U.S. goals and rely primarily on Special Forces, drones, and an increased effort to build up the Afghan National Army to reduce the U.S. footprint in the country over time. By contrast, the counterinsurgency approach, favored by General McChrystal, Gen. David Petraeus, and the Joint Chiefs of Staff, would focus on increasing the Afghan people's sense of security and thus their support for the government in Kabul.

Given the rest of the administration's reluctance to address the issue—a recent *Washington Post* article described Secretary Clinton as "muted" in her comments at a meeting of senior advisers, and noted that Secretary Gates had kept his views "private"—Biden may be the most engaged senior civilian official in this debate.

As Biden so frequently pointed out on the campaign trail, a powerful vice president can be "very dangerous." This is especially the case when a vice president has a track record like Joe Biden's.

The vice president's position on Afghanistan today is a drastic departure from his previous views. In February 2002, Biden said of our effort in that country: "Whatever it takes, we should do it."

The "evolution" of Biden's views since that statement is not out of character. A review of his record on foreign policy in recent decades reveals more discontinuity than coherence.

During the 1980s, Biden opposed funding for the Contras, referring to it as "bankrupt—bankrupt morally, bankrupt politically, and bankrupt militarily." He became a regular opponent of new weapons systems and campaigned against President Reagan's proposed missile defense. An ardent arms-control advocate, in July 1986 Biden chastised President Reagan as "the first president since Dwight D. Eisenhower to not have any success in the arms-control arena." As a presidential candidate in 1987, two years before the fall of the Berlin Wall, Biden praised Soviet premier Mikhail Gorbachev for his "pragmatic leadership" and said that President Reagan was "reacting without a strategy."

Despite that run for the presidency and his position as a senior member of the Senate Foreign Relations Committee, Biden didn't emerge as a key Democratic voice on foreign policy until the 1990s, when he became what Jeffrey Goldberg described in a 2005 article in *The New Yorker* as "a missionary in the cause of armed humanitarian intervention." Biden proudly recounted to Goldberg how he had been on the right side of the debates over Bosnia and Kosovo and how Republicans had opposed efforts to intervene there:

> "I came back to the Republicans and laid out the death camps in Kosovo, the rape camps in Bosnia—I laid it out in stark relief," he told me. "These guys"—the Republicans— "said, 'It's not our business.' What is so transformational in the last four years is that these a**holes who wouldn't give President Clinton the authority to use force" have now become, he said, moral interventionists. "Give me a f**king break."

Biden also advocated the use of U.S. ground forces in Darfur. At a Senate Foreign Relations Committee meeting, Biden said he would "use American force now" and cited the views of senior U.S. military officials that as few as 2,500 U.S. troops could "radically change the situation on the ground." Biden held this belief as late as August of last year.

It's unclear how he has used his powerful West Wing office to promote this policy. Some left-leaning groups recently ran ads in major U.S. newspapers advocating action in Sudan. One cited a Biden remark from July 2008, scolding, "Vice President Biden, it is just a nice quote unless it inspires equally strong action in Sudan."

Also, Biden's views about humanitarian intervention are inconsistent with his views about U.S. strategy in the War on Terror. He has consistently opted for approaches that have later proven wrong, and has shown disregard for the fates of innocent people living under repressive regimes.

He voted with the majority of his Democratic colleagues in the Senate against the first Gulf War. Eleven years later, with many of his fellow Democrats, he supported the Iraq War before turning against it. As late as 2005, he was telling Goldberg that "the decision to go to war was the right one."

In 2006, with violence in Iraq on the rise and some in his party calling for a full-scale withdrawal, Senator Biden began a collaboration with Leslie Gelb, a former president of the Council on Foreign Relations, to promote a truly harebrained scheme to break up Iraq into three autonomous regions. Biden continued to promote the idea until, several years later, the success of the Bush administration's surge (which he had called "absolutely the wrong strategy") exposed his plan for what it was: a ridiculous notion that would likely have destroyed the country and had drastic implications for Iraq's neighbors and U.S. interests in the region.

But that didn't stop Biden. As late as September of last year, he was trying to argue that it was his strategy, not the surge, that had led to success in places such as Anbar Province. He told Tom Brokaw on *Meet the Press* that "they did what I'd suggested two and a half years ago: gave local control."

Biden's attraction to "unique" solutions to complex problems may be behind his fascination with the counterterrorism option in Afghanistan. But his current position on that issue is also starkly different from the one he outlined in statements just a year ago.

Much has been written about Barack Obama's rhetoric on Afghanistan during last year's presidential campaign. He described it as the "central front in the War on Terror." What is often overlooked is that Joe Biden also spoke about the war's importance, often in very personal terms, and attacked John McCain for supposedly taking his eye off of Afghanistan. In September 2008, Biden said:

> John McCain continues to insist, against all the evidence and all the facts, that Iraq is the central front in the war on terrorism. . . . John is more than wrong—he is dangerously wrong.

Biden is now pushing a strategy for that same "central front in the war on terrorism" that is not supported by the commanders on the ground, the combatant commander, or any member of the Joint Chiefs of Staff. It is a strategy that would allow al-Qaeda to return to Afghanistan and would very likely mean the deterioration of Afghanistan to its pre-9/11 condition of Taliban rule.

Oddly, Joe Biden the humanitarian interventionist is nowhere to be found. Commenting in April of this year about a new Afghan law that some felt would allow men to rape their wives, the vice president condemned the law but said, "I am not prepared to send American troops to die for that." Perhaps he should explain why the peoples of Bosnia, Kosovo, and Sudan are more valuable or more vital to U.S. interests.

Like Biden, the Democratic party seems confused about its foreign-policy bearings. Few commentators are comparing the Obama administration to those of the wartime presidents Roosevelt and Truman, or that of Cold Warrior Kennedy. References to LBJ and Carter are far more common. Sweeping statements about America's obligations to those beyond its shores have been set aside as the Obama administration debates the impact of an Afghan surge on the 2010 midterm elections and whether losing Afghanistan to the Taliban would reestablish a haven for al-Qaeda and endanger American security.

With the overwhelming majority of his party's supporters opposing the war in Afghanistan, President Obama's choice in the coming weeks will define his and his party's foreign policy for some time to come. The strategy Vice President Biden now offers, like many others he has advocated over the last three decades, is unsound. To borrow his own words, it would be dangerously wrong. It is divorced from reality and America's most basic national interests. May the president and his party consider these words and ask whether they—like Joe Biden—wish to end up on the wrong side of history once again.

POST-AMERICAN
OBAMA

The Obama Appeal

He's post-racist, but also post-American

By John O'Sullivan

As Republicans watched the recent Democratic debates, the mountainous scale of the problems they face glowered down on them. They were already intimidated by the steepness of the first peak—Mount Change. A mid-January Gallup poll showed that only 17 percent of Americans want to continue with President George W. Bush's policies against a staggering 79 percent who want to change them. All the candidates support "change," of course, but the voters seem to interpret the word in a strongly anti-Republican sense.

The problem only gets worse when they are asked to break down this general desire into support for specific policies. The first four they want to see are: end the war in Iraq/bring the troops home, 26 percent; health-care reform, 19 percent; fix the economy/create more jobs, 18 percent; and secure the borders/address illegal immigration, 10 percent. Three of these four top issues are natural Democratic ones, at least in the closing stages of a GOP administration. The Republican frontrunner would prefer to see the sole Republican issue, immigration, buried because he takes a Democratic view of it. Taxes and fiscal discipline—a couple of natural GOP issues—lag behind, at 7 and 5 percent respectively.

It would be an uphill climb for GOP hopefuls even if they did not have these lead weights strapped to their ankles—because the Democrats, in addition to looking like experienced climbers, seem to be enjoying the exercise. In the South Carolina debate, even former senator John Edwards put on a good show. His schtick as a blow-dried Lear raging against the elemental facts of American middle-class prosperity has worn as thin as a five-and-dime winter coat, and his angry populism lacks the saving grace of humor that Mike Huckabee brings to the same themes; but if he's going—and he is—he intends to go in full ranting mode.

Sen. Hillary Clinton has reestablished herself as the frontrunner. She has done so by the skin of her teeth, and her new status may not survive the South Carolina result; but in recovering, she has shown an unexpected ability to vary her personal style without losing any of her underlying steely resolve. Her "crying game"—whether calculated or a momentary weakness—was extraordinarily successful. It made her less monotonous and more unpredictable. At the same time, she seemed the least vulnerable contender in the debates, displaying the cold sneer of command at some points and a dry wit ("well, that hurts my feelings") at others.

If nominated, she would be a strong opponent, enjoying more or less united Democratic support and media sympathy. But she remains divisive, polarizing, unappealing to independents, and thus the best Democrat the Republicans have got. That is not saying much, however, when all Democrats have an advantage over all Republicans.

CHARM OFFENSIVE

Sen. Barack Obama would plainly be a much stronger candidate in the general election, even if he is at a slight disadvantage in the primaries. In part this is the result of his personality: He is simply likeable. But this likeability goes very deep. He has a kind of cool grace in almost all situations that indicates an underlying self-control remarkable in a relative novice.

This self-control has slipped only once in the campaign, when he responded to Hillary's remarks on her own unlikeability with the line, "You're likeable enough, Hillary." The retort itself was a blunder. It cost him dearly with women voters who felt it to be an unchivalrous putdown. (They had clearly not heard that chivalry is a patriarchal control mechanism.) It may even have sparked a late wave of feminism that still hurts him. But—like other jabs that Obama has delivered in the debates—it indicated an underlying steeliness that is the equal of Hillary's but better concealed.

This blend of charm, grace, and steeliness also influences Obama's ethnic image. One might raid the store of (I trust) inoffensive ethnic stereotypes to describe Obama's personality as a combination of black charm and Swiss efficiency. That in no way intends to suggest that he is running away from an ethnic identity as a black man. Quite the contrary: In his autobiographical works, he embraces such an identity very warmly when he could have presented himself as of "mixed" race. But he is not running as a representative black candidate in the resentful mode of Jesse Jackson or Al Sharpton.

When Obama deals with issues of particular concern to blacks, he stresses their social-justice aspects rather than their specifically racial components. And when he discusses identity issues, he does so as someone advocating an America united on the basis of fairness rather than a racial spoils system. There are illusions and deceptions built into this approach, as we shall see, but his rhetoric and appeal reflect a political identity that rises above race and ethnicity. He is the candidate of a post-racist America.

His electoral support reflects this post-racist appeal. In both New Hampshire and Iowa, he won votes disproportionately from higher-educated voters, young voters, wealthier Democrats, first-time voters, independents, and crossover moderate Republicans. Hillary held on to most of the Democratic base among poorer, less educated, and more partisan Democrats. When all Americans are asked—Gallup again—whether they are optimistic or pessimistic about whether Hillary, Obama, McCain, and Huckabee would bring about real change, Obama scores highest among all Americans as the candidate most likely to effect change. Among Democrats alone, Hillary wins this contest by a large margin. Significantly, both Obama and McCain score well in general because they both have a strong appeal to the other party.

Until recently, Obama's post-racist coalition was both socially upscale and somewhat short on black voters. It included minority professionals who see a black president as a catalyst to remove the few remaining race barriers in the U.S. But the split between strong and marginal Democrats meant that most black voters stayed firmly in Hillary's column.

That is now changing, under three pressures. First, black Democrats who have known and supported Hillary for many years are only now becoming aware of Obama. As they do, some drift into his camp. Second, more blacks are beginning to believe that Obama could actually win the election. And, finally, the Clintons have got entangled in the politics of sensitivity in which they have trapped so many others.

There have been several racially tinged rows of late: whether Hillary cheated Martin Luther King by giving some of the credit for civil-rights reform to LBJ; the reminder by Clinton allies that Obama had used drugs; etc. These have persuaded some black voters that the Clinton campaign is dissing Obama and using racial stereotypes to do so. Both campaigns looked into the abyss of a race row in the Democratic party—and drew prudently back from the brink. But all these factors have, for the moment, pushed black voters of all economic levels toward Obama, widened the social basis of his support, and increased his chances of winning.

NOVEMBER AND BEYOND

How significant would such a victory be? Some commentators after Iowa interpreted the Obama "insurgency" as a final revolutionary push toward a non-racist America. In fact, Obama's success is evidence that such an America was achieved some time ago. Most Americans have long wanted to vote for a black candidate to demonstrate their own lack of prejudice—to themselves as much as to others. If Colin Powell had run for the presidency in 1996, he would probably have defeated Bill Clinton. Twelve years later, an Obama victory would be the celebration of a successful revolution for racial equality rather than the moment when the battle turned.

This sense of "change" already achieved explains why veteran black activists like Jesse Jackson and Al Sharpton have been so nervous about the Obama campaign: A black man in the White House would undermine the politics of white guilt/black exploitation that has long been their stock in trade. It also helps explain why Obama's campaign has such a joyful, relaxed, and oddly uncontroversial "feel" to it. On the morrow of Iowa, it seemed almost an apolitical celebration; though the New Hampshire defeat later cooled the celebration, it did not alter its nonpartisan quality of complacent moral self-congratulation. It is not a very bold prediction to say that if Obama gets his party's nomination, the post-Iowa mood that America had a moral responsibility to elect Obama will be restored on steroids.

Two main obstacles, however, stand between him and the nomination. The first is the gender gap. Hillary scored well among women long before New Hampshire. Last year Gallup showed that she had a strong favorability rating not only among Democratic women but also among independent women. In New Hampshire she defeated Obama by 46 to 34 percent. Polls since then show her retaining a strong lead over Obama even among black women.

Hillary has been a strong, partisan defender of feminist positions for many years; she is now reaping the reward for that. But the apparent last-minute swing of women voters into her column suggests something else at work too: a collective *amour-propre*. Many women felt that the first woman to be a serious presidential candidate was being unfairly dismissed from consideration before a single primary had been held by a cast of establishment characters that included Obama himself ("You're likeable enough, Hillary"). That sharpened the sexual resentments and loyalties of women beyond the ranks of feminism that secured her victory. Such feelings will inevitably fade in time; they may be offset among black women by racial resentments aroused by the King brouhaha; for the moment, however, they persist and complicate Obama's electoral calculations.

The second obstacle is the growing divide between blacks and Hispanics in U.S. politics. By and large this has developed without the mass media's noticing, because the press has a liberal vision of all minorities cooperating harmoniously under a Rainbow Umbrella. But it emerged unmistakably in the Nevada caucuses, when Hillary won big among Hispanics and Obama among blacks; and the polls show a similar divergence nationwide and in primaries such as Florida's. It arises directly from the growth of the Hispanic community, which is itself driven largely by immigration. As Steven Malanga demonstrates in the current *City Journal*, this has resulted in a loss of economic opportunities and political power among black Americans—and in their substantial internal migration. In Los Angeles, the black population fell by 123,000 in the last 15 years, while the Hispanic one rose by more than 450,000. Whole areas of the cities have changed their ethnic character. The employment rate of unskilled black males has declined considerably as a result. And immigration policy is becoming the focus of disagreement between the two communities.

This creates some difficulty for a Democratic coalition that contains both. As it happens, Hillary and Obama are united in supporting a comprehensive immigration reform that would include amnesty for the illegal workers already here. Both campaigns will seek to reduce controversy over the issue now and until November. Hillary in particular is conscious that if she is the Democratic nominee, and if John McCain is *not* the GOP's nominee, then the Republicans could split the Democrats and detach a larger-than-usual segment of the black vote by campaigning to reduce immigration levels. Obama has meanwhile played his part by urging in a church sermon that black Christians have a duty to welcome immigrants. But both are uncomfortably aware that the Hispanic-black split over immigration is an issue that at any moment could go critical—and deny one of them the prize.

Obama's strategic difficulties largely dissolve, however, once he wins the nomination. All the women's groups, led by Hillary, would support him against any conceivable Republican. No substantial number of black Americans, however concerned about immigration, would pass up the chance to elect the first black president. Ditto most liberal Democrats. And almost all Obama's other recent actions have strengthened his appeal to independents and crossover Republicans. His recent praise for Reagan wrong-footed his opponents, strengthened his crossover appeal, widened his ideological options, and confirmed his public image of cool graciousness. Not a bad return on saying what almost everyone, including Hillary and Bill, knew to be an admirable platitude.

More important even than that is his recent rhetoric on American unity. Obama has mastered the lost art of delivering patriotic speeches that sound sincere and sensible. Such rhetoric used to be a Republican specialty, but liberal opinion long ago bullied them out of it ("super-patriotism"), and now they have lost the knack. The American people retain a taste for patriotic unity, however, and will likely respond to it with added respect when it comes from a post-racist black American.

But there are two kinds of American unity: the natural unity of citizens with equal rights, and the managed unity of groups with equal rights. These are in direct conflict with each other. Obama's rhetoric is undoubtedly sincere, but it gives the impression that he favors the first sort of unity when he actually wants to ratify and advance the second. A glimpse at his speeches and programs demonstrates that he is committed, like all the Democratic candidates, to such policies as racial preferences, multiculturalism, liberal immigration laws, and the transfer of power from America's constitutional republic to non-accountable global bodies and international law. For Obama is not merely a post-racist; he is a post-nationalist and a post-American too. But will the eventual Republican nominee be able to explain the difference?

May 5, 2008

Unified Theory

The candidate of change forbids you to disagree

By Jonah Goldberg

'**U**nity is the great need of the hour," insists Barack Obama. Unity and the hope for unity and the need for unity in the pursuit of hope and the hope that our unified hopefulness will carry us to ever greater heights of hopeful unity until each and every one of us is the person he longs to be: That's what Barack Obama is all about. And don't you *dare* say otherwise. These are not "just words."

One might be forgiven for asking, What the heck do these words *mean?* Specifically, what's so special about unity? Unity for what? Unity around what? Obama has an answer: We need unity "not because it sounds pleasant or because it makes us feel good, but because it's the only way we can overcome the essential [empathy] deficit that exists in this country." His wife, Michelle, dilates on the subject: "We have to compromise and sacrifice for one another in order to get things done. That is why I am here, because Barack Obama is the only person in this who understands that. That before we can work on the problems, we have to fix our souls. Our souls are broken in this nation."

If you go on to read or listen to more of this stuff, you'll eventually see what they're getting at: Americans need to rally around Obama and his platform if they are going to mend their souls and make this a better country. You might buy this or you might think it's hogwash, and there's no shortage of arguments out there for both perspectives, but what is it with this obsession with *unity?* American politicians used to have a word to describe their appeals to collective action for the betterment of the whole society. They called it *patriotism*. But that word summons the banshees of the Democratic party. To raise the issue of patriotism, say the Democrats, is to question whether someone is patriotic at all—at least when Republicans do it.

Except that Republicans don't actually use the word "patriotism" very much. Nevertheless, Democrats hear it in almost everything Republicans say. When Republicans disputed John Kerry's commitment to national defense, Democrats said they were questioning his patriotism. When John McCain released an ad calling himself the "American president Americans have been waiting for," one could hear outraged caterwauling from the Democratic jungle: *What's John McCain trying to say? We're un-American? Who's he calling unpatriotic?* Fred Barnes, writing in *The Weekly Standard,* calls this anticipatory offense "patriotism paranoia." Indeed, there does seem to be psychological insecurity on display. If I say to a male friend, "Those are nice shoes," and he responds with "How dare you call me gay!" it's fair to say he's the guy with the issues.

Obama himself has gotten in on this act: "In this campaign, we will not stand for the politics that uses religion as a wedge and patriotism as a bludgeon." His campaign manager, David Plouffe, chimed in later: "Questioning patriotism is something we don't think has a place in this campaign."

This is a mess. Barack Obama and other Democrats use the word "unity" as a substitute for something like "patriotism." They consider "questioning the patriotism" of Democrats—even when it's not actually being questioned—beyond the pale and "divisive." All the while they use the word "divisive" with diuretic abandon as code for "unpatriotic." And if that's not confusing enough, many Democrats routinely declare flat-out that Republicans are unpatriotic. For example, Howard Dean, when running for president, insisted that John Ashcroft was "not a patriot. John Ashcroft is a direct descendant of Joseph McCarthy." John Kerry complained that Bush's "creed of greed" led him to "unpatriotically" allow corporations to move overseas. And what is the "chickenhawk" epithet if not an attack on the patriotism of war supporters who do not enlist, lubricated with the spittle of anti-hypocrisy hysteria?

Perhaps we should "unpack" some of these concepts, as the academics say.

DEFINITIONS GOOD AND BAD

Suppose there were someone who believed it might do America "a ton of good to have our butts kicked" (in the words of left-wing novelist Tom Robbins). Or that the world would benefit from "a million Mogadishus," and that "the only true heroes are those who find ways to defeat the U.S. military" (Columbia professor Nicholas De Genova). Or that America is "just downright mean"—brimming with "broken souls"—and hasn't done anything worthy of pride in her lifetime (Michelle Obama). Or that because of the racism of "U.S. of KKK A" at home, and its cruelty abroad, we shouldn't sing "God bless America" so readily as "God damn America" (Rev. Jeremiah Wright). It would stretch the bounds of neither reason nor decorum to say these people are less in love with America than is your typically patriotic person. Try replacing "America" in the above quotes with just about any other noun. "The only true heroes are those who find ways to defeat the New York Yankees!" "Cleveland is downright mean!" "God damn my KKK-car!" And so on. In any of these instances, a reasonable person might question the speaker's love for the Yankees, Cleveland, or Chrysler. But no reasonable person may ever—*ever!*—question someone's love of country when he attacks it with similar words.

If patriotism is a thing, if it has meaning as a concept and as a description of attitudes or behaviors, it isn't surprising that some people will be more patriotic than others—whatever definition we finally settle on. And we need not settle on just one, because there are many kinds of patriotism. Walter Berns argues in his book *Making Patriots* that, because America is a nation founded on individual rights, American patriotism differs markedly from, say, Spartan patriotism, which extolled loyalty to the collective and the state above all else. Many liberals would agree with this at first blush. But they can't seem to hold on to the idea that American patriotism has something to do with *America*.

John Edwards, whose bifocal vision of "two Americas" involves pity for one and contempt for the other, says, "Patriotism is about refusing to support something you know is wrong, and having the courage to speak out with strength and passion and backbone for something you know is right." Well, no. Dissent is about all that. Patriotism is about loving your country. So, yes, dissent *could* be patriotic—or it could be treason. Everyone from American Communist spies and saboteurs dedicated to the overthrow of the U.S. government during the Cold War to the protesters carrying signs saying "Bomb Texas, Not Iraq" at your typical ANSWER rally is patriotic, according to Edwards's definition, which is 200-proof nonsense.

Or consider this supposedly brilliant bumper-sticker insight: "Dissent is the highest form of patriotism." Mark Steyn has had great fun with that line, pointing out that Thomas Jefferson—usually credited as its author—never said anything of the sort. Steyn traces the fakery back to a 1991 quote from Nadine Strossen, the head of the ACLU, an organization with a vested interest in putting the founders' imprimatur on relentless knee-jerk complaining. (The oldest reference I can find in major newspapers is a 1969 line from New York mayor John Lindsay, who was congratulating anti-Vietnam protesters at Columbia for their patriotism. He was booed after he left the stage, and Paul Boutelle—a cab driver and Socialist Workers party mayoral candidate known after 1979 as Kwame Montsho Ajamu Somburu—vilified him in absentia. The crowd loved it.)

It is worth pointing out that if Jefferson had in fact said something like that, he would have been what social scientists call a *moron*. As John O'Sullivan once noted, tongue firmly in cheek, "Dissent is the highest form of patriotism. Treason is the highest form of dissent. Therefore treason is the highest form of patriotism." Yet when you listen to the verbal contortions many on the left go through to defend the *New York Times*'s efforts to reveal national-security secrets, or to journalists who think expressing open sympathy for America in the international arena is a grave sin, or simply to the usual battiness of countless America-haters, you can appreciate the wisdom of the Italian proverb that the truest things are said in jest.

Like the layers of steel in a Japanese sword, the logic of "Jefferson's" wisdom folds in on itself until one is left with an adamantine blade of invincible ignorance and razor-sharp asininity. For example, if George Bush and conservatives are little better than Prussian heel-clickers for wearing their patriotism on their sleeves, what does it say about you when you wear your patriotism on your bumper? After all, "Dissent is the highest form of patriotism" is bandied about almost exclusively by self-styled dissenters. "This is not the first time in American history when patriotism has been distorted to deflect criticism and mislead the nation," harrumphed the Great Dissenter John Kerry in 2006. "No wonder Thomas Jefferson himself said: 'Dissent is the greatest form of patriotism.'" Get it? John Kerry is bragging about what a great *patriot* he is by calling attention to what a wonderful *dissenter* he is. "I am more patriotic than thou" sneaks up on us in the Trojan Horse of "I dissent more than thou."

Now it must be said that no conservative standing upon the shoulders of Burke, Nock, Buckley, Hayek, Goldwater, and Reagan would for a moment dispute the suggestion that dissent *for the right reason* can be *one* high form of patriotism. But it depends on the reason. The dissenter-for-dissent's-sake is among the most common species of pest in the human ecosystem. The reflexive contrarian who cares not what he is contradicting is quite simply the most useless of citizens.

When confronted with the assertion that the Soviet Union and the United States were moral equivalents, William F. Buckley Jr. famously responded that if one man pushes an old lady into an oncoming bus and another man pushes an old lady out of the way of a bus, we should not denounce them both as men who push old ladies around. Likewise, we should not say that the man who dissents from a church-burning mob and the man who dissents from a fire brigade are morally equivalent "dissenters."

"FASCIST," YOU SAY?

Part of the problem is that many on the left think patriotism is essentially fascist, another name for nationalism and jingoism. And some may use it that way—but some may also call a duck a "cat," which doesn't mean we should all be hostage to this usage. The misuse of "patriotism" and "dissent" is worse, because a country without a word to describe its love for what is best within it is a country ill-equipped to defend what is best within it. And, for the record, it should be noted that fascism wasn't about patriotism, but nationalism. Hitler himself insisted he was no patriot, but a nationalist. In the United States, a creedal nation dedicated to limited government and individual rights, fascist nationalism is almost the complete opposite of patriotism.

Alas, that's too much for many liberals to process, so they have come to extolling the word "unity." But here's the thing: Unity by itself has no moral worth whatsoever. The only value of unity is strength, strength in numbers—and, again, that *is* a fascist value. That's the symbolism of the *fasces*, the bundle of sticks that in combination are invincible. Rape gangs and lynch mobs? Unified. The mafia? Unified. The SS? They had unity coming out the yinyang. Meanwhile, Socrates, Jesus, Thomas More, and an endless line of nameless souls were dispatched from this earth in the name of unity. Returning to Buckley, the mob that pushes old ladies in front of a bus and the posse that tries to stop the mob are not morally equivalent. Indeed, the lone man who faces the mob with justice on his side is the greatest of heroes.

American patriots pay heed: The founding fathers dedicated a great deal of thought to the subject of unity, and they found it was something to view with skepticism at best and, more often than not, with fear. Hence we have a constitution designed to thwart the baser forms of unity. Our government is set up so that the Senate cools the populist passion of the House, the executive thwarts the passions of the legislature and vice versa, and the Supreme Court checks the whole lot, to which its composition is in turn ultimately subject. "Divisiveness"—the setting of faction against faction, one branch of government against another, and the sovereignty of the individual above the group—was for the founders the great guarantor of our liberties and the source of civic virtue.

Rightly ordered unity in a democratic republic is the end result of ceaseless debate and discussion. But today, ceaseless debate and discussion is precisely what many liberals object to. As Al Gore is fond of saying about global warming, "The time for debate is over." Legions of liberals insist that we must move beyond ideology and partisan differences on this, that, and the other. But have you ever heard anyone say that we need to "move beyond ideology" for the sake of bipartisan unity and then abandon his own position? Of course not. When someone says that we need to get past labels and move beyond ideology, what he means is that you need to drop your principled objections and get with the program. That is why *Time* magazine heralded Arnold Schwarzenegger and Michael Bloomberg as "new action heroes": These "post-partisans" had dropped any pretense of a Republican vision and simply embraced the liberal agenda. That's what the AARP intends when its ad campaign for health-care reform proclaims: "Divided we fail." The mascot for this campaign is a chimera, the GOP elephant's head and the Democratic jackass's body. Of course, such a creature cannot be created without shrinking the Republican brain or vastly inflating the Democratic ass.

The fact that we take liberals seriously when they talk about patriotism doesn't mean they are doing the same. John Edwards wouldn't call a Communist saboteur a patriot, and Barack Obama's love of unity would hardly drive him to praise the virtue of the mob. But what's important to understand is that it is the Left, not the Right, that speaks in code. The supposedly neutral language of "unity" and "division" is not neutral at all. "My rival in this race," Obama proclaimed early in 2007, "is not other candidates. It's cynicism." His insistence that "divisiveness" is his greatest enemy is belied by the fact that he is unwilling to repudiate Jeremiah Wright, who is about as divisive a character as we've seen in American politics in a generation. Meanwhile, Obama sees nothing wrong with demonizing Geraldine Ferraro—or even his own grandmother—for crass political purposes. He uses seemingly conciliatory language to give the impression that he is above the fray, transcendent and enlightened. Only those who see through his act are cynical, only those who disagree with his agenda are divisive. But he won't name names, because that would spoil the illusion. "It would," in the words of Andrew Ferguson, "at last be plain that his politics of unity, his politics of 'addition not subtraction,' is simply another way of recasting the old 'politics of us vs. them' that he says he disdains."

It's worth asking, then: If Obama and the Democrats believe *unity* in all things is the supreme political value, but the American tradition holds that *liberty* is a greater good, then could it not be argued that Barack Obama's rival in this race is not the other candidates, but patriotism?

May 5, 2008

The Obama Way

A Chicago pol's special brand of insincerity

By Fred Siegel

Political campaigning necessarily produces a wide gap between words and deeds—this is the price of bringing together a broad coalition with disparate interests. All effective politicians are at times authentically insincere or sincerely inauthentic. Exaggeration, embellishment, overstatement, double-talk, systematic deception, and lies presented as metaphorical "truths" are the order of the day.

So of course Barack Obama is no different. He exaggerates the credit he deserves for a very limited piece of ethics-reform legislation. He embellishes when he presents himself as having had a consistent record on the Iraq War, when in fact he's done a fair amount of zigzagging. He engages in double-talk when, on NAFTA and Iraq, he tells the rubes one thing and the policy people another. He overstates when he presents his minimal accomplishments in the Illinois senate as proof of his stature. He engages in systematic deception when he says he doesn't take money from lobbyists. He presents a lie as metaphorical truth when he says it was the 1965 "Bloody Sunday" attacks on peaceful civil-rights protesters in Selma, Ala., that inspired his parents to marry (they had been married for years already).

All of this is unappealing, but also unexceptional. What makes Obama different is that there's not just a gap but a chasm between his actions and his professed principles—this would normally kill a candidacy. And because his deeds are so few, the disparity is all the more salient. Obama, far more than the others, is the "judge me by what I say and not what I do" candidate. He wants to be the conscience of the country without necessarily having one himself.

The disparity between Obama's rhetoric of transcendence and his conventional Chicago racial and patronage politics is a leitmotif of his political career. In New York, politicians (Reverend Al excepted) are usually forced to pay at least passing tribute to universal principles and the ideal of clean government. But Chicago, until recently a city of Lithuanians, blacks, and Poles governed by Irishmen on the patronage model of the Italian Christian Democrats, is the city of political and cultural tribalism.

Blacks adapted to both the tribalism and the corrupt patronage politics that accompanied it. Historically, one of the ironies of Chicago politics is that the clean-government candidates have been the most racist, while those most open to black aspirations have been the most corrupt. When the young Jesse Jackson received his first audience with Richard Daley the elder, the mayor—impervious to the universalism of the civil-rights movement in its glory—offered him a job as a toll-taker. Jackson thought the offer demeaning but in time adapted. In Chicago, racial reform has meant that today's Mayor Daley has been cutting blacks in on the loot. Louis Farrakhan, Jesse Jackson, Jeremiah Wright, and Barack Obama are all, in part, the expression of that politics. It hasn't always worked for Chicago, which, under the pressure of increasing taxes to pay for bloated government, is losing its middle class. But it has served the city's political class admirably.

For all his Camelot-like rhetoric, Obama is a product, in significant measure, of the political culture that *Chicago Tribune* columnist John Kass described thus: "We've had our chief of detectives sent to prison for running the Outfit's (i.e., the mob's) jewelry-heist ring. And we've had white guys with Outfit connections get $100 million in affirmative action contracts from their drinking buddy, Mayor Richard Daley. . . . That's the Chicago Way." At no point did Obama, the would-be savior of American politics, challenge this corruption, except for face-saving gestures as a legislator. He was, in his own Harvard Law way, a product of it.

Why, you might ask, did the operators of Chicago's political machine support Obama? Part of the answer was given long ago by the then-boss of Chicago, Jake Arvey. When asked why he made Adlai Stevenson—a man, like Obama, more famous for speeches than for accomplishments—his party's gubernatorial candidate in 1948, Arvey is said to have replied that he needed to "perfume the ticket."

Obama first played a perfuming role as a state senator. His mentor, Emil Jones, the machine-made president of the senate, allowed him to sponsor a minor ethics bill. In return, Obama made sure to send plenty of pork to Jones's district. When asked about pork-barrel spending, Jones famously replied, "Some call it pork; I call it steak."

Obama repaid the generosity. When he had a chance to back "clean" Democratic candidates for president of the Cook County board of supervisors and Illinois governor, he stayed with the allies of the Outfit. The gubernatorial candidate he backed, Rod Blagojevich, is now under federal investigation, in part because of his relationship with Tony Rezko, the man who helped Obama buy his current house.

The Chicago Way has delivered politically for Obama even this year. Ninety percent of his popular-vote lead over Hillary Clinton comes from Illinois, and two-thirds of that 90 percent comes just from Cook County. Some of this advantage came from the efforts of Obama's political ally, the flame-throwing reverend James Meeks, a political force in his own right. Meeks, who mocks black moderates as "niggers," is an Illinois state senator, the pastor of a mega-church, and a strong supporter of Jesse Jackson's powerful political operation, which has put its vote-pulling muscle squarely behind the Obama campaign.

It was only with Obama's remarks about "bitter," white, working-class, small-town voters that we saw his difficulties appealing beyond the machine's reach. He won his U.S. Senate race in 2004 not only because his opponents self-destructed, but also because of the machine's ability to deliver votes (this minimized his need to campaign among working-class whites downstate). In Pennsylvania he has lacked such assistance—and the campaigning has not gone nearly so well. First Obama pretended to be a bowler and scored a 37. Then, appearing before a supposedly closed San Francisco audience, he complained that small-town Pennsylvanians "cling to guns or religion or antipathy toward people who aren't like them, or anti-immigrant sentiment or anti-trade sentiment, as a way to explain their frustrations."

This is the man who belongs to a church built around bitterness, rancor, and conspiratorial fear. During the Reverend Wright affair, Obama not only repeatedly lied about what he knew and when, but violated the spirit of the civil-rights movement in its mid-1960s glory. When as a young man I was on the periphery of the movement, there was an unwritten rule that if people told racist jokes or speakers engaged in defamatory rhetoric, you needed to register your immediate disapproval by confronting the speaker or ostentatiously walking out.

Wright's "black theology" is essentially a Christianized version of Malcolm X's ideology of hate. But for 20 years Obama, who had planned to run for mayor of Chicago, kept silent about the close if at times competitive relationship between Reverend Wright, whose 8,000-member mega-church gave him his political base, and Louis Farrakhan. His ambition overrode his moral integrity.

As part of his "black value system," Reverend Wright attacked whites for their "middle classism," "materialism," and "greed in a world of need." Obama sounded similar notes in his recent address at the Cooper Union, in which he laid the blame for the sub-prime mortgage crisis on those who had "embraced an ethic of greed, corner cutting, and inside dealing." But that's exactly what Obama did in buying his luxurious house. Given the choice of purchasing a less expensive home or getting into bed with his fundraiser-cum-slumlord-cum-fixer Tony Rezko, Obama chose the latter. Then again, the oppressed of Trinity Church are building Wright a $1.6 million, 10,340-square-foot home complete with four-car garage, whirlpool, and butler's pantry. This house, which backs onto a golf course, is to sit in Tinley Park, a gated community that is 93 percent white.

The Obamas' charitable giving is consistent with Reverend Wright's talking left while living right. Obama and his wife are quite well-off. They had an estimated income of $1.2 million from 2000 to 2004. But the man who preaches compassion and mutuality gave all of 1 percent of that income to charity during those years. Most of that went to subvent Wright's church.

BELOW THE FRAY

There is a similar chasm when it comes to Obama's claim to post-partisanship. His achievements in reaching out to moderate voters are largely proleptic. But words are not deeds, and while Obama has few concrete achievements to his name, his voting record hardly suggests an ability to rise above Left-versus-Right. In the Illinois state senate he made a specialty of voting "present," but after his first two years in the U.S. Senate, *National Journal*'s analysis of roll-call votes found that he was more liberal than 86 percent of his colleagues. His voting record has only moved farther left since then. The liberal Americans for Democratic Action now gives him a 97.5 percent rating, while *National Journal* ranks him the most liberal member of the Senate. By comparison, Hillary Clinton, who occasionally votes with the GOP, ranks 16th. Obama is such a down-the-line partisan that, according to *Congressional Quarterly*, in the last two years he has voted with the Democrats more often than did the party's majority leader, Harry Reid.

Likewise, for all his talk of post-racialism, Obama has, with the contrivance of the press, played traditional South Side racial politics. The day after his surprise loss in New Hampshire, and in anticipation of the South Carolina primary, with its heavily black electorate, South Side congressman Jesse Jackson Jr.—Obama's national co-chairman—appeared on MSNBC to argue, in a prepared statement, that Hillary Clinton's teary moment on the campaign trail reflected her deep-seated racism. "Those tears," said Jackson, "have to be analyzed. . . . They have to be looked at very, very carefully in light of Katrina, in light of other things that Mrs. Clinton did not cry for, particularly as we head to South Carolina, where 45 percent of African Americans will participate in the Democratic contest. . . . We saw tears in response to her appearance, so that her appearance brought her to tears, but not Hurricane Katrina, not other issues." In other words, whites who are at odds with, or who haven't delivered for, Chicago pols can be obliquely accused of racism on the flimsiest basis, but pillars of local black politics such as Reverend Wright, with his exclusivist racial theology, are beyond criticism.

Liberals love Obama's talk of taking on powerful financial interests. But here too he is rather slippery. In his Cooper Union speech, he denounced in no uncertain terms the "special interests" of people on Wall Street (who are well represented among his campaign donors). He of course had an opportunity to push for repealing the privileged tax treatment of private-equity firms when that question was before Charles Grassley's Senate subcommittee—but he simply made a pro forma statement in favor of doing so and disappeared into the woodwork. Nationally, as in Chicago, Obama the *soi-disant* "reformer" never crosses swords with any of his putative foes. To pick another example, he has attacked "predatory" sub-prime lenders while taking roughly $1.3 million in contributions from companies in that line of business.

Obama is the internationalist opposed to free trade. He is the friend of race-baiters who thinks Don Imus deserved to be fired. He is the proponent of courage in the face of powerful interests who lacked the courage to break with Reverend Wright. He is the man who would lead our efforts against terrorism yet was friendly with Bill Ayers, the unrepentant 1960s terrorist. He is the post-racialist supporter of affirmative action. He is the enemy of Big Oil who takes money from executives at Exxon-Mobil, Shell, and British Petroleum.

Obama has, in a sense, represented a new version of the Invisible Man, a candidate whose color obscures his failings. Perhaps his remarks about bitter Pennsylvanians' clinging to their guns have finally made visible the real man and his Harvard hauteur.

But so far, the wild discrepancy between Obama's words and his deeds, and between his enormous ambitions and his minimal accomplishments, doesn't seem to have fazed his core supporters, who apparently suffer from a severe case of cognitive dissonance. Like cultists who rededicate themselves when the cult's prophecies have been falsified, his fans redouble their delusions in the face of his obvious hypocrisy. That is because Obama, in the imagination of many of his fans in the public and the press, is both a deduction from what was—the failures of the Bush administration and the scandals of the Clintons— and an expression of what should be. The ideal, the aspiration, is so rhetorically appealing that it has been assumed to be true. They remind one of Woodrow Wilson's answer when asked if his plan for a League of Nations was practicable: "If it won't work, it must be made to work."

March 23, 2009

Prime Minister Obama

Will European statism supplant the American way?

By Mark Steyn

Back during the election campaign, I was on the radio and a caller demanded to know what I made of the persistent rumor that Barack Obama was born in Kenya. "I doubt it," I said. "It's perfectly obvious he was born in Stockholm. Okay, maybe Brussels or Strasbourg." And the host gave an appreciative titter, and I made a mental note to start working up a little "Barack Obama, the first European prime minister to be elected president of the United States" shtick for maybe a year into the first term.

But here we are 20 minutes in, and full-scale Europeanization is already under way: Europeanized health care, Europeanized daycare, Europeanized college education, Europeanized climate-change policy . . . Obama's pseudo-SOTU speech was America's first State of the European Union address, in which the president deftly yoked the language of American exceptionalism to the cause of European statism. Apparently, nothing testifies to the American virtues of self-reliance, entrepreneurial energy, and the can-do spirit like joining the vast army of robotic extras droning in unison: "The government needs to do more for me." For the moment, Washington is offering Euro-sized government with Euro-sized economic intervention, Euro-sized social programs, and Euro-sized regulation. But apparently not Euro-sized taxation.

Hmm. Even the Europeans haven't attempted that trick. But don't worry, if that pledge not to increase taxes on families earning under $250,000 doesn't have quite the Continental sophistication you're looking for in your federal government, I doubt it will be operative very long.

Most Americans don't yet grasp the scale of the Obama project. The naysayers complain, *Oh, it's another Jimmy Carter*, or *It's the new New Deal*, or *It's LBJ's Great Society applied to health care*. You should be so lucky. Forget these parochial nickel'n'dime comparisons. It's all those multiplied a gazillionfold and nuclearized—or Europeanized, which is less dramatic but ultimately more lethal. For a distressing number of American liberals, the natural condition of an advanced, progressive Western democracy is Scandinavia, and the U.S. has just been taking a wee bit longer to get there. You've probably heard academics talking about "the Swedish model" and carelessly assumed they were referring to the Britt Ekland retrospective on AMC. If only. And, incidentally, fond though I am of Britt, the fact that I can think of no Swedish dolly bird of the last 30 years with which to update that gag is itself a telling part of the problem. Anyway, under the Swedish model, state spending accounts for 54 percent of GDP. In the U.S., it's about 40 percent. Ten years ago, it was 34 percent. So we're trending Stockholmwards.

And why stop there? In Scotland, Northern Ireland, and Wales, government spending accounts for between 72 and 78 percent of the economy, which is about the best a "free" society can hope to attain this side of complete Sovietization. Fortunately for what's left of America's private sector, "the Welsh model" doesn't have quite the same beguiling euphony as "the Swedish model." Even so, if Scandinavia really is the natural condition of an advanced democracy, then we're all doomed. And by "doomed" I'm not merely making the usual overheated rhetorical flourish in an attempt to persuade you to stick through the rather dry statistics in the next paragraph, but projecting total societal collapse and global conflagration, and all sooner than you think.

There are two basic objections to the wholesale Europeanization of America. The easy one is the economic argument. The short version of late-20th-century history is that Continental Europe entirely missed out on the Eighties boom and its Nineties echo. A couple of weeks back, the evening news shows breathlessly announced that U.S. unemployment had risen to 7 percent, the highest in a decade and a half. Yet the worst American unemployment rate is still better than the best French unemployment rate for that same period. Indeed, for much of the 1990s the EU as a whole averaged an unemployment rate twice that of the U.S. and got used to double-digit unemployment as a routine and semi-permanent feature of life.

Germany, the economic powerhouse of Europe in the Sixties and Seventies, is now a country whose annual growth rate has averaged 1.1 percent since the mid-Nineties; where every indicator—homeownership, new car registrations—is heading down; and in which government agencies have to budget for such novel expenditures as narrowing the sewer lines in economically moribund, fast-depopulating municipalities because the existing pipes are too wide to, ah, expedite the reduced flow. Even flushing yourself down the toilet of history is trickier than it looks.

Of course, if you're one of the seemingly endless supply of Americans willing to turn up at the president's ersatz "town meetings" to petition the seigneur to take care of your medical bills and your mortgage and the gas in your tank, the Euro-deal looks pretty sweet. When they deign to work, even the French can match the Americans in hourly productivity. Unfortunately for boring things like GDP, the Euro-week has far fewer hours. There are government-mandated maximum 35-hour workweeks, six weeks of paid vacation, more public holidays, and, in the event that, after all that, some unfortunate clerical error still shows the calendar with an occasional five-day week, you can always strike. The upshot is that, while a working American puts in an average 1,800 hours a year, a working German puts in 1,350 hours a year—or 25 percent less.

It's tempting to assume these are deeply ingrained cultural differences. "It's the good life, full of fun, seems to be the ideal," as the Gallic crooner Sacha Distel smoothly observed. But, in fact, until the Seventies Americans and Europeans put in more or less identical work hours. What happened is that the Protobamas of the Continental political class legislated sloth, and, as is the way, the citizenry got used to it.

Indeed, the proposed European Constitution enshrines leisure as a fundamental right. Article II-91: "Every worker has the right to limitation of maximum working hours, to daily and weekly rest periods and to an annual period of paid leave." There's no First Amendment or Second Amendment, but who needs free speech or guns when life is one gentle swing in the government hammock?

When American commentators notice these numbers, it's usually to crank out a "Why oh why can't we be as enlightened?" op-ed. A couple of years back Paul Krugman wrote a column asserting that, while parochial American conservatives drone on about "family values," the Europeans live it, enacting policies that are more family-friendly. On the Continent, claims the professor, "government regulations actually allow people to make a desirable tradeoff—to modestly lower income in return for more time with friends and family."

As befits a distinguished economist, Krugman failed to notice that, for a continent of "family friendly" policies, Europe is remarkably short of families. While America's fertility rate is more or less at replacement level—2.1—seventeen European nations are at what demographers call "lowest low" fertility—1.3 or less, a rate from which no society in human history has ever recovered. Germans, Spaniards, Italians, and Greeks have upside-down family trees: Four grandparents have two children and one grandchild. The numbers are grim, and getting grimmer. The EU began the century with four workers for every retiree. By 2050, Germany will have 1.1 workers for every retiree. At Oktoberfest a decade or three hence, that fetching young lad in the lederhosen serving you your foaming stein will be singlehandedly propping up entire old folks' homes. Except he won't. He'll have scrammed and headed off to Australia in search of a livelier youth scene, or at any rate a livelier late-middle-aged scene. And the guy taking his place in the beer garden won't be wearing lederhosen because he'll be Muslim and they don't like to expose their knees. And, come to think of it, he's unlikely to be serving beer, either. The EU would need at least another 50 million immigrants—working immigrants, that is (they're not always, especially with Euro-welfare)—to keep wrinkly old Gerhard and Jean-Claude in the social programs to which they've become accustomed.

To run the numbers is to render them absurd: It's not about economic performance, public-pensions liabilities, entitlement reform. Something more profound is at work. Europe has entered a long dark Oktoberfest of the soul, drinking to oblivion in the autumn of the year, as *les feuilles mortes* pile up all around.

Let's take the second part of Paul Krugman's assertion: These "family friendly" policies certainly give you "more time." For what? High-school soccer and 4-H at the county fair? No. As we've seen, kids not called Muhammad are thin on the ground. God? No. When you worship the state-as-church, you don't need to bother showing up to Mass anymore.

Civic volunteerism? No. All but extinct on the Continent. So what do Europeans do with all that time? Do they paint, write, make movies? Not so's you'd notice. Not compared with 40 years ago. Never mind Bach or even Offenbach, these days the French can't produce a Sacha Distel or the Germans a Bert Kaempfert, the boffo Teuton bandleader who somewhat improbably managed to play a critical role in the careers of the three biggest Anglophone pop acts of the 20th century—he wrote "Strangers in the Night" for Sinatra, "Wooden Heart" for Elvis, and produced the Beatles' first recording session. If that sounds like a Trivial Pursuit answer, it's not. Eutopia turned out to be the trivial pursuit; to produce a Bert Kaempfert figure right now would be a major cultural accomplishment Europe can't quite muster the energy for. "Give people plenty and security, and they will fall into spiritual torpor," wrote Charles Murray in *In Our Hands*. "When life becomes an extended picnic, with nothing of importance to do, ideas of greatness become an irritant. Such is the nature of the Europe syndrome."

The key word here is "give." When the state "gives" you plenty—when it takes care of your health, takes cares of your kids, takes care of your elderly parents, takes care of every primary responsibility of adulthood—it's not surprising that the citizenry cease to function as adults: Life becomes a kind of extended adolescence—literally so for those Germans who've mastered the knack of staying in education till they're 34 and taking early retirement at 42 (which sounds a lot like where Obama's college-for-all plans will lead).

Genteel decline can be very agreeable—initially: You still have terrific restaurants, beautiful buildings, a great opera house. And once the pressure's off it's nice to linger at the sidewalk table, have a second café au lait and a pain au chocolat, and watch the world go by. At the Munich Security Conference in February, President Sarkozy demanded of his fellow Continentals: "Does Europe want peace, or do we want to be left in peace?" To pose the question is to answer it. Alas, it works only for a generation or two, and then, as the gay-bar owners are discovering in a fast-Islamifying Amsterdam, reality reasserts itself.

In 2003, the IMF conducted a study of Eurosclerosis and examined the impact on chronic unemployment and other woes if the Eurozone labor market were to Americanize—that's to say, increase participation in the work force, reduce taxes and job-for-life security, etc. The changes would be tough, but over the long term beneficial. But it's too late for that: What's "changed" is the disposition of the people: *If it's unsustainable, who cares? As long as they can sustain it till I'm dead.* That's the second and most critical objection to Europeanization: It corrodes self-reliance very quickly, to the point where even basic survival instincts can be bred out of society in a generation or two. In *America Alone* I cited a headline that seemed almost too perfect a summation of a Continent where entitlement addiction trumps demographic reality: "Frenchman Lived with Dead Mother to Keep Pension." She was 94 when she croaked, so she'd presumably been getting the government check for a good three decades, but hey, it's 700 euros a month. He kept her corpse under a pile of newspapers in the living room for five years and put on a woman's voice whenever the benefits office called. Since my book came out, readers have sent me similar stories on a regular basis: "An Austrian woman lived with the mummified remains of her aunt for a year, Vienna police said Wednesday." In Europe, nothing is certain except death and welfare, and why let the former get in the way of the latter?

It's interesting that it never occurred to the IMF that anyone would be loopy enough to try their study the other way around—to examine the impact on America of Europeanization. For that, we had to wait for the election of Barack Obama. Which brings us to the third problem of Europeanization: What are the consequences for the world if the hyper-power embarks on the same form of assisted suicide as the rest of the West? In quite the wackiest essay Foreign Policy has ever published, Parag Khanna of the Brookings Institution argued that the European Union was now "the world's first metrosexual superpower." And he meant it as a compliment. Mr. Khanna's thesis is that, unlike the insecure American cowboy, Europe is secure enough in its hard power to know when to deploy a little sweet-smelling soft power. Seriously:

> The EU has become more effective—and more attractive—than the United States on the catwalk of diplomatic

clout. . . . Metrosexuals always know how to dress for the occasion (or mission) . . . but it's best done by donning Armani pinstripes rather than U.S. Army fatigues. . . . Even Turkey is freshening up with *eau d'Europe.* . . . Stripping off stale national sovereignty (that's *so* last century), Europeans now parade their "pooled power," the new look for this geopolitical season. . . . Brand Europe is taking over. . . . Europe's flashy new symbol of power, the Airbus 380, will soon strut on runways all over Asia.

But don't be deceived by the metrosexual superpower's pleatless pants—Europe hasn't lost touch with its hard assets. . . . Europe's 60,000-troop Rapid Reaction Force will soon be ready to deploy around the world. . . . Just as metrosexuals are redefining masculinity, Europe is redefining old notions of power and influence. Expect *Bend It Like Brussels* to play soon in capital cities worldwide.

And on and on, like one of those pieces an editor runs when he wants to get fired and go to Tuscany to write a novel. The Airbus 380 is a classic stillborn Eurostatist money pit, the Rapid Reaction Force can't deploy anywhere beyond a Europe Day parade down the Champs-Élysées, and given that the governing Socialist caucus on the Brussels city council already has a Muslim majority I doubt they'll be bending it themselves that much longer.

This is the logical reductio of the Robert Kagan thesis that Americans are from Mars, Europeans are from Venus. It's truer to say that Europeans are from Pluto, which was recently downgraded to "dwarf planet" status. In foreign affairs, a dwarf superpower doesn't have policies, it has attitudes—in part because that's all it can afford. An America that attempts Euro-scale social programs would have to reel in its military expenditures. After all, Europe could introduce socialized health care and all the rest only because the despised cowboy across the ocean was picking up the tab for the continent's defense. So for America to follow the EU down the same social path would have huge strategic implications for everyone else, not least Europe. We would be joining the Continentals in prancing around in Armani pinstripes and *eau d'Europe* as the bottom dropped out of our hard assets. And Putin, Kim

Jong Il, the mullahs, et al. might not find the perfume as heady as Mr. Khanna does.

Even in their heyday—the Sixties and Seventies—the good times in Europe were underwritten by the American security guarantee: The only reason France could get away with being France, Belgium with being Belgium, Sweden with being Sweden is that America was America. Kagan's thesis—Americans are from Mars, Europeans are from Venus—will look like paradise lost when the last conventional "great power" of Western civilization embraces the death-cult narcissism of its transatlantic confreres in the full knowledge of where that leads. Why would you do anything so crazy? Ah, but these are crazy times: Europeans are from Pluto, Americans are from Goofy.

REAL
OBAMA

December 3, 2007

Cut from the Same Cloth

Jimmy Carter in the '76 campaign, Barack Obama in this one

By Richard Lowry

Barack Obama comes from a long line of thoughtful, achingly idealistic reformers in Democratic presidential politics. They inspire people, impress everyone with their resplendent good intentions, eschew rough-and-tumble politics as usual—and lose.

In a *Los Angeles Times* column, Ronald Brownstein traces the archetype from Eugene McCarthy in 1968 to Gary Hart in 1984 to Bill Bradley in 2000. He writes, "Since the 1960's, Democratic nominating contests regularly have come down to a struggle between a candidate who draws support primarily from upscale, economically comfortable voters liberal on social and foreign policy issues, and a rival who relies mostly on downscale, financially strained voters drawn to populist economics and somewhat more conservative views on cultural and national security issues." Obama fits the losing pattern so exactly he should be tempted to abandon all hope—audacious or not—right now.

And yet, there's a counterexample of this kind of reformer prevailing in which Obama can take some comfort—one James Earl Carter Jr.

Carter wasn't really in the McCarthy-Hart-Bradley mold. He ran a conservative, or at least an ideologically indistinct, race in the 1976 Democratic primaries. He was cagey about his abortion views, but basically pro-life; relatively conservative on economics; and somewhat supportive of right-to-work laws. (As all the qualifiers suggest, he was hard to pin down on anything). Liberals distrusted him just because he was a southerner. He vied for the George Wallace vote and benefited from four major candidates—Morris Udall, Birch Bayh, Fred Harris, and Sargent Shriver—dividing liberal support.

So Carter doesn't refute Brownstein's insight. Indeed, in the New Hampshire primary, he attracted blue-collar and middle-class volunteers, not the college-student activists that other Democratic candidates typically relied on. But Obama and Carter represent an uncanny thematic continuity; if you put aside ideology, the content of their campaigns is almost identical. There has been a lively competition among analysts to identify the year—1948? 1968? etc.—to which current circumstances in the War on Terror and in our politics are most analogous. Barack Obama should hope it's 1976, when the country turned to a hope-hawking political neophyte to soothe away memories of an unpopular war and fundamental doubts about the capacities and intentions of the United States government.

No historic analogy is exact, of course. Jimmy Carter, the prototypical darkhorse, began his primary campaign in 1975 in obscurity as a former one-term Georgia governor. He helped invent the Iowa caucuses as a significant step to the nomination. (So new was the national press attention there that the chairman of the Iowa Democrats charged people to watch star TV correspondents like CBS's Roger Mudd do their caucus-night reports.) Carter's team realized the potential of an Iowa strategy after he was warmly received at a retirement dinner for the Plymouth County recorder in February 1975. From then on, they considered coverage in the *Des Moines Register* more important than the *Washington Post*. Carter had an insatiable appetite for retail campaigning and sometimes would show up unannounced at people's homes. If they weren't there, he'd leave a note explaining he had dropped by.

Obama, by contrast, was shot out of a cannon of hype and publicity earlier this year. If he had attempted to leave a note on anyone's door at the inception of his campaign, he would have been swamped by starstruck admirers, and TV satellite trucks would have clogged the neighborhood.

But Carter and Obama have essential similarities. First, there is the sheer implausibility of their presidential ambitions. Carter's aides were at first embarrassed by the idea of even talking about him running for president. In his classic account of the 1976 campaign, *Marathon*, Jules Witcover twice uses the word "audacity" to describe Carter's decision to run—exactly the word Obama used to describe his own presidential ambitions in his announcement speech.

Carter at least had four years of executive experience, although he still had to stretch for presidential-seeming credentials. He talked about his work at a "nuclear power plant as a nuclear physicist" (an exaggeration) and his trade missions abroad as Georgia governor. This is just as lame and implausible as Obama's touting his work as a community organizer and law professor—a *constitutional*-law professor, he's always careful to add—as preparation for the presidency. Incredibly enough, Obama has cited his major in international relations at college as foreign-policy experience. Neither man, by rights, had any business launching presidential campaigns. Both men, however, are fiercely competitive strivers who know how to wear their ambitions lightly.

Prior to the 1976 race, one of Carter's aides urged him in a memo to "capitalize on your greatest asset—your personal charm." It's easy to forget, now that Carter has covered himself in the shame of so many outrageous post-presidential statements and acts, that charisma was the rocket fuel of Carter's candidacy. During TV appearances, political chronicler Theodore White writes, "his smile went on as soon as the camera's red light flashed, as if he were plugged in." He converted supporters. Witcover refers to Carter's interactions with individual voters as "personal political baptisms." Witcover recounts an event in New Hampshire with seventh- and eighth-graders that Carter ended by raising up his arms and saying, "I love all of you." The kids rose up and surrounded Carter, who began picking up and hugging them one by one. "Suffer the little children to come unto me," commented one reporter, awed by what he was seeing.

MR. SMOOTH

Personal charm is the very basis of Obama's candidacy; without it—given his lack of accomplishments, experience, and defining issues—he wouldn't be running. He's undeniably a winsome guy, smart and smooth: the coolest major politician in recent memory. His candidacy is given a special frisson of excitement because he's the first-ever black candidate who has a real chance of winning the White House. If the size of his events precludes him from having a Carter-like laying of hands on children, the press corps has swooned into his arms like those kids into Carter's. One of the strongest arguments he makes in behalf of his candidacy is essentially that he's more likable than Hillary and therefore won't engender the fierce opposition of the other side.

Carter didn't get by on charm alone. His theme of hope and change hit exactly the right notes in a post-Vietnam, post-Watergate America yearning for a fresh start. His mantra, repeated over and over again, was, "I want a government that is as good, and honest, and decent, and truthful, and fair, and competent, and idealistic, and compassionate, and as filled with love as are the American people." He would achieve it partly through his own qualities as a person and a candidate. He said in one of his commercials, "There are lots of things I would not do to be elected. Listen to me: I'll never tell a lie. I'll never make a misleading statement. I'll never betray the confidence any of you has in me."

Of course, Obama talks about hope so often he could almost trademark the word. And he speaks of change just as much, trying to tap into a public feeling of discontent running nearly as deep as when Carter ran. In his Jefferson-Jackson Day dinner speech in Iowa, Obama advocated "a party that doesn't just offer change as a slogan, but real, meaningful change—change that America can believe in," adding—in case someone didn't get the point—"that's why I am running for the Presidency of the United States of America: to offer change that we can believe in." Like Carter, Obama offers himself as the embodiment of this kind of change, the new bottle into which to pour a new politics beyond the tired baby-boomer conflicts and the acrimony of the Bush-Clinton-Bush years.

Carter in 1976 and Obama today present themselves as non-politician politicians willing to trample on political conventions. Carter aide Hamilton Jordan told Witcover the idea was "for somebody to stand up and tell the American people to do the things that were unpopular, a feeling that if politicians dealt more openly with the electorate that they would respond well." In his Jefferson-Jackson Day speech, Obama said almost exactly the same thing. There is an opportunity to bring the country together, according to Obama, "and that is why the same old Washington textbook campaign just won't do in this election. That's why not answering questions 'cause we are afraid our answers won't be popular just won't do. That's why telling the American people what we think they want to hear instead of telling the American people what they need to hear just won't do."

This all tends to run to vaporous abstraction. When the media tried to pin Carter down on issues, Witcover writes, "he dismissed the insistence on clear-cut responses by saying that reporters asked him 'frivolous' questions that the public really didn't care about." Earlier in Obama's campaign, before he saw opportunity in attacking Hillary Clinton for not being specific enough, he struck the same note. At a meeting of the Democratic National Committee he said, "There are those who don't believe in talking about hope. They say, 'Well, we want specifics; we want details; and we want white papers; we want plans.' We've had a lot of plans, Democrats. What we've had is a shortage of hope."

Carter tried to have a trans-ideological appeal. Witcover writes, "Why should a candidate be liberal or conservative down the line, [Carter] argued, when most of the American people were not?" Obama made much the same case in his book *The Audacity of Hope*. He has quoted Martin Luther King for the proposition, "It's not either/or, it's both/and." On *Meet the Press* recently, he rued the fact that people tend "to argue along the spectrum of you're either a hawk or a dove." He also touted his "ability to focus on getting the job done, as opposed to getting embroiled in ideological arguments."

Both Carter and Obama clothe their appeals to trans-ideological change in Christian religiosity. Jimmy Carter had what Hamilton Jordan called "a weirdo factor" because he was a born-again Christian who spoke frankly talking about his faith at a time when people weren't used to that. Carter was unabashed in talking about love—his line to those eighth-graders about loving all of them wasn't exceptional. Obama is running in an environment inured to candidates talking about their faith. But part of his appeal as a Democrat is how effortlessly he talks about religion. In his famous 2004 convention speech, he used Biblical imagery to powerful effect. He too invokes love, if not as frequently as Carter. At a church service in South Carolina, he told the congregation, "I am confident that we can create a kingdom right here on earth."

A MASSIVE SELF-REGARD
The danger in a candidate who runs against the political system on the

basis of his ability to embody and deliver change sold in religion-infused terms is a massive self-regard. Carter demonstrated it at every turn. Witcover writes, "Carter had a distinct way of converting his every act, even a refusal to give a plain answer to a plain question, into an act of political morality. This pretension in him often rankled, but he never hesitated to invoke it if it served his purpose." Obama has the same tendency. He has been intensely focused on the ethics and processes of his own campaign and deflects criticisms of him as the old politics and the status quo biting back at him because of his unique righteousness.

Obama's attack on Hillary Clinton is instructive. She has said she wants a bipartisan commission to examine the financing of Social Security before she commits herself to anything. Obama criticizes this as unacceptable politics as usual. What's his alternative? Well, as he told Tim Russert, "I will convene a meeting as president where we discuss all of the options that are available." Obama speaks more favorably of increased payroll taxes than Hillary, but otherwise there's not much daylight between them. He nonetheless inflates this into a yawning difference of principle because if he holds a position it, ipso facto, is part of the new politics; if someone else holds it, it's the grubby politics of old. Obama can't help, by the very nature of his candidacy, believing in a self-centered Obama-ism above all else.

Comparing anyone to Jimmy Carter feels like an attack because Carter was a failed president who went on to a post-presidential career of great obnoxiousness. But Carter, obviously, won his party's nomination and the general election. Obama could do the same. One difference between the mood among Democrats in 1976 and now is that back then the dragon had been slain in the form of Richard Nixon. Today's dragon, George W. Bush, still lives, so the Democratic base hungers less for Jimmy Carter–like national healing than for Howard Dean–like recrimination. As Obama has begun to pick up a little against Hillary, his message has taken on an angrier edge, while—somewhat discordantly—he has preserved old lines about uniting the country.

Would Obama be as ineffectual a president as Carter? There's no way to know. He needn't, obviously, have Carter's managerial weaknesses, or his poisoned relations with Congress. But there was something inherent in Carter's campaign, and the conceit behind it, that played into his failure. Theodore White notes, "He arrived in Washington having won both his nomination and his election on personality alone." He got stiffed legislatively, having, in White's words, "ignored his Congress, as sinners and politicians."

All presidential candidates think highly of themselves. The personal messianism of a Carter or Obama, though, sets them up to divide the world into acolytes and enemies—Carter's undoing. Obama would feel the same pull. He would be positioned as the self-anointed savior of Washington, an act that would quickly wear thin on Capitol Hill, especially if—as he probably would—Obama takes it seriously.

Carter's signal failures were in foreign affairs. So much of foreign policy is judgment and execution, there's no way to know in advance how Obama would perform. But he seems to have Carter's foreign-policy DNA. Carter saw hostility directed at the United States around the world—even by our sworn enemies—as the result of our own actions, and thought he could lure the Soviet Union out of its aggression through self-abasing gestures and reassuring diplomatic patter. On Iran, Obama has all the same instincts, blaming its aggression around the Middle East on our bullying behavior, forswearing the use of our troops in Iraq to try to check Iranian ambitions within that country, and promising unconditional talks from which the Iranians would surely grab ever more "carrots" because none of Obama's "sticks" would be plausible. Carter complained of our "inordinate fear of Communism"; does Obama believe we have an inordinate fear of Islamofascism?

If Hillary Clinton has her way, we'll never need to find out. Unlike Carter, Obama has an establishment frontrunner standing in his way. Vanquishing her will be hard, but if he does, Obama will believe all the more in the world-shaking newness of his candidacy. The example of Jimmy Carter says, to the contrary, we've been here before, and it wasn't a happy experience.

June 30, 2008

The Organizer

What did Barack Obama really do in Chicago?

By Byron York

C*hicago*—Barack Obama often cites his time as a community organizer here in Chicago as one of the experiences that qualify him to hold the nation's highest office. "I can bring this country together," he said in a debate last February. "I have a track record, starting from the days I moved to Chicago as a community organizer."

When Obama says such things, the reaction among many observers is: *Huh?*

Audiences understand when he mentions his years as an Illinois state legislator, or his brief tenure in the U.S. Senate. But a community organizer? What's that?

Even Obama didn't know when he first gave it a try back in 1985. "When classmates in college asked me just what it was that a community organizer did, I couldn't answer them directly," Obama wrote in his memoir, *Dreams from My Father*. "Instead, I'd pronounce on the need for change. Change in the White House, where Reagan and his minions were carrying on their dirty deeds. Change in the Congress, compliant and corrupt. Change in the mood of the country, manic and self-absorbed. Change won't come from the top, I would say. Change will come from a mobilized grass roots."

If you substitute "Bush" for "Reagan," you have a fairly accurate description of Obama's 2008 campaign. That's not a coincidence; it suggests that something about community organizing was central to Obama's world view back then, and has remained central to his development as the politician he is today. What was it?

I counted myself among those who didn't have a good idea of what a community organizer does. So I came here to learn more about

Obama's time in the job, from 1985 to 1988. What did he *do?* What did he accomplish? And what in his experience here stands as a qualification to be president of the United States?

THE RADICAL'S RULES

Perhaps the simplest way to describe community organizing is to say it is the practice of identifying a specific aggrieved population, say unemployed steelworkers, or itinerant fruit-pickers, or residents of a particularly bad neighborhood, and agitating them until they become so upset about their condition that they take collective action to put pressure on local, state, or federal officials to fix the problem, often by giving the affected group money. Organizers like to call that "direct action."

Community organizing is most identified with the left-wing Chicago activist Saul Alinsky (1909-72), who pretty much defined the profession. In his classic book, *Rules for Radicals*, Alinsky wrote that a successful organizer should be "an abrasive agent to rub raw the resentments of the people of the community; to fan latent hostilities of many of the people to the point of overt expressions." Once such hostilities were "whipped up to a fighting pitch," Alinsky continued, the organizer steered his group toward confrontation, in the form of picketing, demonstrating, and general hell-raising. At first, the organizer tackled small stuff, like demanding the repair of streetlights in a city park; later, when the group gained confidence, the organizer could take on bigger targets. But at all times, the organizer's goal was not to lead his people anywhere, but to encourage them to take action on their own behalf.

Alinsky started in the 1930s with workers in the Chicago stockyards. Many years later, when Obama arrived here, he came from a different perspective.

"Barack had been very inspired by the civil-rights movement," Jerry Kellman, the organizer who hired Obama, told me recently. "I felt that he wanted to work in the civil-rights movement, but he was ten years too late, and this was the closest he could find to it at the time." Obama, in his memoir, put it more simply when he said he went to Chicago to "organize black folks." Kellman, a New Yorker who had gotten into organizing in the 1960s, was trying to help laid-off factory workers on the far South Side of Chicago. He led a group, the Calumet Community

Religious Conference, that had been created by several local Catholic churches. The Calumet region—basically the farthest southern reaches of Chicago plus the suburbs in northern Indiana—was an industrial area that had been hard hit by the closings of Wisconsin Steel and other industries. Kellman and the churches hoped to get some of those jobs back.

But there was a problem in the Chicago part of the equation. The area involved, around the Altgeld Gardens housing project and the neighborhood of Roseland, was nearly 100 percent black. Kellman was white, as were others who worked for CCRC. "The people didn't open up to him like they would to somebody who was black and really understood what was going on in their lives," Yvonne Lloyd, one of the key "leaders"—that is, local residents who worked closely with Obama—told me. "Black people are very leery when you come into their community and they don't know you." Lloyd and another leader, Loretta Augustine-Herron, insisted that Kellman hire a black organizer for a new spinoff from CCRC to be called the Developing Communities Project, which would focus solely on the Chicago part of the area.

So Kellman set out to find a black organizer. He ran an ad in some trade publications, and Obama responded. But at first Kellman wasn't sure Obama was right for the job. "My wife was Japanese-American," Kellman recalled. "I showed her the résumé, with the background in Hawaii. The name's Obama, so I asked, 'Could this be Japanese?' She said, 'Sure, it could be.'" It was only when Kellman talked to Obama on the phone, and Obama "expressed interest in something African-American culturally," that a relieved Kellman offered Obama the job.

But Kellman had to sell Obama to the leaders. "Jerry introduces Barack, and Barack is so young, it's like, 'Oh my God,'" Loretta Augustine-Herron remembered. Obama was obviously smart, and he wanted to be an organizer, but he was, in fact, quite young (24) and he didn't actually know much about the job. Despite those drawbacks, he seemed to work some sort of magic on the leaders. "He had a sensitivity I have never seen in anybody else to this day," Augustine-Herron told me. "He understood." The women were sold. "He didn't have experience," Augustine-Herron said. "But he had a sensitivity that allowed us to believe that he could do the job." So Obama it was.

WHAT'S YOUR SELF-INTEREST?

New to Chicago, Obama set about conducting dozens of one-on-ones, that is, individual interviews with South Side residents in which he tried to discover which issues were most important to them. "You have to understand a person's self-interest—that's Alinsky's terminology," Mike Kruglik, an organizer who worked with Kellman and Obama, told me. "What's happened to that person in his or her life? Where are they going? Why are they going there? What are they really passionate about?"

After the initial interviewing, Obama went to work on a number of projects.

The long-term goal was to retrain workers in order to restore manufacturing jobs in the area; Kellman took Obama by the rusted-out, closed-down Wisconsin Steel plant for a firsthand look. But the whole thing was a bit of a pipe dream, as the leaders soon discovered. "The idea was to interview these people and look at education, transferable skills, so that we could refer them to other industries," Loretta Augustine-Herron told me as we drove by the site of the old factory, now completely torn down. "Well, they had no transferable skills. I remember interviewing one man who ran a steel-straightening machine. It straightened steel bars or something. I said, well, what did you do? And he told me he pushed a button, and the rods came in, and he pushed a button and it straightened them, and he pushed a button and it sent them somewhere else. That's all he did. And he made big bucks doing it."

That, of course, was one of the reasons the steel mill closed. And it became clear that neither Obama nor Kellman nor anyone else was going to change the direction of the steel industry and its unions in the United States. Somewhere along the line, everyone realized that those jobs wouldn't be coming back. So Obama looked for new opportunities. One thing he spent a lot of time on was creating a network of contacts beyond the white Catholic priests who originally sponsored the Developing Communities Project. "Many of the parishes were in predominantly African-American communities, and I think all of the priests were non-African-American," Rev. Alvin Love, head of the Lilydale First Baptist Church on 113th Street, told me. "Barack came to me and wanted to try to connect with the whole community."

Trying to construct a wide-ranging alliance of churches, Obama succeeded with Love and a few other ministers, but he was hampered by the fact that he didn't go to church himself. "I said, 'If you go to a pastor, and you ask him to come get involved in a community effort, and you say you have a group of churches, and that pastor asks you what church you belong to, and you say none—then it's hard to get that pastor on board,'" Love recalled telling Obama. "He said, 'I know, I understand, I'm working on it.' He said, 'I believe, I'm just waiting for the right spot, the right place, the right time.'" Love wasn't the only minister to bring that up with Obama, and before long Obama, drawn to the preaching of Rev. Jeremiah Wright, joined Trinity United Church of Christ on 95th Street—where he would stay until political pressure created by Wright's anti-American outbursts, combined with the anti-white message from another Obama friend, South Side priest Michael Pfleger, led him to resign his church membership.

Obama got the ministers involved in several projects, without great success. There was a push to get more city money for South Side parks after the Justice Department told the Chicago Park District it had to spend more on minority neighborhoods. There were plans for afterschool programs, and job retraining for adults. But if you ask Obama's fellow organizers what his most significant accomplishments were, they point to two ventures: the expansion of a city summer-job program for South Side teenagers and the removal of asbestos from one of the area's oldest housing projects. Those, they say, were his biggest victories.

'WE JUST FOUND OURSELVES AN ISSUE'

If you start in Chicago's downtown Loop area, and drive south on the Bishop Ford Expressway, you'll come to the 130th Street Exit amid an almost surreal landscape. To the left, there is the massive Continental Grain elevator complex, looming like a cluster of skyscrapers, with a rusting tanker moored nearby in the Calumet River. Not far away are a number of rotting, shut-down businesses. Farther south, there is the Waste Management CID Landfill, a vast, and growing, mountain of garbage. And to the right, there is the Calumet Water Reclamation Plant, better known as the sludge plant, treating sewage from all around the region. And in the middle of it all is Altgeld Gardens, a sprawling brick low-rise housing project built in the 1940s in what is probably the least people-friendly location one could ever imagine.

Loretta Augustine-Herron lived here for a while in the 1960s, and one day in May she took me around in her pickup truck. In those days, she said, there was an awful smell coming across 130th Street from the sludge plant. "Sometimes when the wind blew the wrong way, you could not take a deep breath," she said. "It was horrible." And isolated, too: Then, as now, there were no stores, or restaurants, or much of anything in easy walking distance of Altgeld. You can't take a train, because there are none around. And you can forget about a taxi. The best way to get around is the bus, which makes regular runs through the complex. Still, the sense of isolation is considerable.

Near the back of the Altgeld complex is a tightly locked gymnasium and a low, brown-brick building closed in by a chain-link fence, topped in places with barbed wire. It is Our Lady of the Gardens church, where Augustine-Herron and Yvonne Lloyd met, and where they got to know Barack Obama. And it was here that much of his career as an activist was set.

A staple priority of organizers like Obama was the summer-jobs program. In the 1980s the jobs were administered by the Mayor's Office of Employment and Training, or MET, but the nearest MET office to Altgeld was a long way away—beyond 95th Street—and located in what some felt was enemy territory. "Our children, in order to get those summer-job programs, had to go over to the East Side—Vrdolyak's territory," Yvonne Lloyd told me, referring to Edward "Fast Eddie" Vrdolyak, the Chicago alderman who was the champion of white ethnics and a sworn enemy of Harold Washington, the black mayor whose presence had inspired blacks across the city, including Obama.

"So, if you're living in Altgeld, you don't have the bus fare to go way over there, and they were out of their element, and they ended up not getting the jobs." Why not demand a job center in their neighborhood? In *Dreams from My Father*, Obama describes visiting MET headquarters and looking at a brochure listing the locations of all branch offices. There was nothing south of 95th Street. "This is it," he said. "We just found ourselves an issue."

Obama then choreographed a drive to demand a new MET office.

(The point, remember, was not for him to make the demands but for the leaders to do it for themselves.) They set up a meeting with MET officials, and then Obama drilled the leaders on what they should say. He took them around Roseland looking for a possible site for the new office. They found a shut-down department store at Michigan Avenue and 110th Street, and located the building's owners. "He did all the legwork for us and brought it back to us," Lloyd told me, "and we went downtown to the offices of the store and negotiated." In a climactic meeting at Our Lady of the Gardens—Obama had, once again, carefully rehearsed the leaders on what they should say—MET officials agreed to open the new office. Obama had an accomplishment to point to.

"Our kids were able to go there, sign up, and get their summer jobs," Lloyd told me. "It was fantastic to me, I just felt like—oh, it meant so much to us." They were thrilled beyond words when Harold Washington himself came to the ribbon-cutting for the new office.

BATTLE OVER ASBESTOS

The other Obama accomplishment most people mention is the asbestos cleanup at Altgeld. One day someone—it's not clear who—noticed that some rather specialized work seemed to be going on at the management office in the center of the complex. "A young lady came to us and said they've got white suits on and they're doing something in the office," Yvonne Lloyd told me. "We asked them what they were doing and they said, 'We're renovating.' That didn't sound right. Why would they be wearing all this gear if they were just renovating?" It turned out the workers were removing asbestos from the building.

In Obama's telling, the problem was discovered when a young woman noticed a small-print notice in the classified section of a newspaper, soliciting bids for asbestos cleanup at Altgeld. However it began, it didn't take the residents long to guess that if asbestos was in the office, it might be in their apartments, too. That discovery led to Obama's greatest hit as an organizer.

Obama recruited the young woman to pay a visit to the Chicago Housing Authority official who worked at the management office. Obama went too, hoping the official would deny that there was any asbestos in the apartments. "A cover-up would generate as much publicity as the asbestos, I had told myself," Obama wrote in *Dreams from My Father*. "Publicity would make my job easier." And sure enough, the CHA official denied it all. Obama followed up—had the residents follow up, of course—with letters to top CHA officials. Finally, the group sent a message to the agency's executive director, warning they would show up at his office to demand action. They got in touch with local TV stations, and everyone came to cover the asbestos showdown.

As it turned out, there was no showdown. CHA officials accommodated the protesters, promising to begin testing the Altgeld apartments for asbestos that very day. They also promised to attend a meeting at Our Lady of the Gardens to listen to everyone's concerns. A few weeks later, the director of CHA himself came to the church's gymnasium, where Obama's group was prepared to present a demand for timely repairs. Perhaps 300 people came, along with the TV crews. Things veered toward fiasco when the young woman Obama had chosen to question the CHA director wouldn't give up the microphone so the director could answer. A semi-comic tug-of-war ensued, with the director finally bolting the meeting, followed by an increasingly angry crowd.

It was a fiasco, and racial conspiracy theories quickly spread among the residents. "The whole thing was put together by Vrdolyak," Obama quotes one man saying. "You saw that white man egging the folks on. They just trying to make Harold look bad." Obama was deflated; at the very least, the big show was a setback to his effort. It was precisely the sort of scene he had wanted to avoid. "He said, 'Don't get confrontational, don't raise your voice, don't scream and holler,'" Yvonne Lloyd told me. "He said, 'You'll get more the other way.'" (Jerry Kellman told me that Obama was not "a straight Alinsky organizer," and his advice to Lloyd at Altgeld suggests that he generally preferred to avoid overt confrontation.)

The organizers ended up winning anyway, although the cleanup wasn't finished until years later. But something had changed for Obama during the asbestos fight, and he began to consider leaving Chicago for law school. As he looked back, he believed that, on one hand, he had trained some good people; Loretta Augustine-Herron, for example, told me he inspired her to go to college, which led her to a satisfying career. But on the other hand, Obama seemed to realize that it was very, very hard to get anything done. "He didn't see organizing making any significant changes in things," Jerry Kellman recalled.

The solution, Obama felt, was to find a way to political power of his own.

"He was constantly thinking about his path to significance and power," Mike Kruglik told me. "He said, 'I need to go there [Harvard Law School] to find out more about power. How do powerful people think? What kind of networks do they have? How do they connect to each other?'"

In a few months, Obama was gone. He had been an organizer for three years. When he returned to Chicago after law school, he did some voter-registration work and then joined a civil-rights practice. In 1996, he ran for the state senate. Eight years later, he was elected to the U.S. Senate, and within a year after that he was exploring a run for president.

THE ORGANIZER

We look to formative experiences to help us understand presidential candidates. Visit an aircraft carrier in wartime and you'll learn something about John McCain. Pilots fly off the deck, and sometimes they come back, and sometimes they don't. One day, McCain didn't, and began the time as a prisoner of war that both revealed his character and launched his political career. No matter what he has done since, the U.S. Navy is the culture that made McCain, with his heavy emphasis on duty, honor, and country.

Community organizing is just as essential in understanding Obama. But what does it say about him?

The first thing is that he has a talent for, well, organizing. Everyone who worked with Obama says he was good at the job. And he has used the techniques he learned in Chicago to organize his own presidential campaign, going so far as to enlist Mike Kruglik to help start a "Camp Obama" program to instill organizing principles into Obama supporters. The result is a campaign that even Obama's opponents admit is a very impressive operation.

But Obama's time in Chicago also revealed the conventionality of his approach to the underlying problems of the South Side. Is the area crippled by a culture of dysfunction? Demand summer jobs. Push for an after-school program. Convince the city to spend more on this or that. It was the same old stuff; Obama could think outside the box on ways to organize people, but not on what he was organizing them *for*.

Certainly no one should live in an apartment contaminated by asbestos, but Obama did not seem to question, or at least question very strongly, the notion that the people he wanted to organize should be living in Altgeld at all. The place was, after all, one of the nation's capitals of dysfunction. "Every ten years I would work on the census," Yvonne Lloyd told me. "I always had Altgeld. When you look at those forms from the census, you had three or four generations in one apartment— the grandmother, the mother, the daughter, and then her baby. It was supposed to be a stepping stone, but you've got people that are never going to leave." No doubt Obama would agree that that is a bad thing, but when a real attempt to break through that culture of dysfunction—the landmark 1996 welfare-reform bill, now widely accepted as one of the most successful domestic-policy initiatives in a generation—came up, Obama vowed to use all the resources at his disposal to undo it. "I made sure our new welfare system didn't punish people by kicking them off the rolls," he said in 1999. Two years earlier, he had declared: "We want to make sure that there is health care, child care, job training, and transportation vouchers—everything that is needed to ensure that those who need it will have support." Obama applied his considerable organizational skills to perpetuating the old, failed way of doing things.

Obama's professional colleagues, people like Jerry Kellman, believe his lasting accomplishment was to build an organization, the Developing Communities Project, that survived his departure. Today, DCP still exists, run out of a small Methodist church building on 95th Street, working on after-school programs, drug prevention, and voter registration. It has become, much more than it was when Obama was there, a grant-getting institution; according to tax records, about three-quarters of its funding comes from government grants, with the rest from liberal foundations like the Woods Fund, on whose board Obama sat from 1993 to 2002.

Has any of that brought about the change Obama spoke of back in 1985? Not in any large sense. But if Obama doesn't have much to show for his years as an organizer, it's fair to say that many of the people he touched revere him deeply. Remember what Loretta Augustine-Herron said: Obama had such a powerful presence that he made her *believe* he could do the job, even though there was little in his résumé to suggest he could. Does that sound familiar to anyone who has watched the Obama campaign? When hope is the product, Obama can sell it with the best of them.

When he left for law school, Obama wondered what he had accomplished as an organizer. He certainly had some achievements, but he did not—perhaps could not—concede that there might be something wrong with his approach to Chicago's problems. Instead of questioning his own premises, he concluded that he simply needed more power to get the job done. So he made plans to run for political office. And in each successive office, he has concluded that he did not have enough power to get the job done, so now he is running for the most powerful office in the land.

And what if he gets it? He'll be the biggest, strongest organizer in the world. He'll dazzle the country with his message of hope and possibility. But we shouldn't expect much to actually get done.

September 1, 2008

Who Is Barack Obama?

His autobiography paints a disturbing picture

By Michael Gledhill

Who is Barack Obama? Obama the presidential candidate presents himself as a man who has loved America from his earliest childhood, a man proud of his mixed-race roots who comfortably transcends polarized racial politics, a man who eschews the ideologies of Left and Right, an optimistic healer. But in his critically acclaimed autobiography, *Dreams from My Father: A Story of Race and Inheritance*, Obama is something else entirely.

Obama published his autobiography in 1995, when he was in his mid-thirties. Unlike most books by politicians, which are concoctions of clichés penned by ghostwriters, *Dreams* was clearly written by Obama himself. Unlike most politicians, Obama can write and loves language. (He was contemplating a career as a novelist at the time he wrote *Dreams*.) Most important, Obama wrote his autobiography after he had become a political activist but before he was a politician; the book is therefore candid in a way a conventional politician's memoir would never be.

Dreams is a complex, introspective book. Its theme is how Obama, born in Hawaii to a white student mother and Kenyan student father, grows to view himself and the white society around him. The Obama of *Dreams* abandons his multiracial roots to forge an alienated black identity—that of a man steeped in radical ideology who views history in terms of a huge chasm separating oppressor from oppressed, white from black, and rich from poor; a man who is never more emotionally at home than when sitting in the church pew listening to Rev. Jeremiah Wright rant about white racism.

People and politicians change, and the Obama of today may not be the one of 13 years ago. But he has never forsworn *Dreams* or given a detailed explanation of how he has evolved since writing it. The book thus remains an extraordinary window into Obama.

WHAT DOES HE LIKE ABOUT AMERICA?

Candidate Obama claims that "throughout my life, I have always taken my deep and abiding love for this country as a given." He tells us his "heart swells with pride at the sight of our flag."

In *Dreams*, his heart swells at many things but sight of the flag certainly isn't one of them. There he presents a warts-only history of the U.S., a story of evil and suffering. U.S. society is a "racial caste system" where "color and money" determine where you end up in life. He tells us of white children's stoning black children, Jim Crow, and heatless Harlem housing projects. He describes "Japanese families interned behind barbed wire; young Russian Jews cutting patterns in Lower East Side sweatshops; dust-bowl farmers loading up their trucks with the remains of shattered lives."

Obama says the Hawaiian islands, where he grew up, are beautiful, but quickly reminds us that behind the beauty lurks the "ugly conquest of the native Hawaiians . . . crippling disease brought by missionaries . . . the indenturing system that kept Japanese, Chinese, and Filipino immigrants stooped sunup to sunset in [the fields]."

Candidate Obama proudly tells audiences that his white grandparents were raised in the American heartland. But in *Dreams* he describes this heartland as the "landlocked center of the country, a place where decency and endurance and the pioneer spirit were joined at the hip with conformity and suspicion and the potential for unblinking cruelty."

Candidate Obama fondly tells audiences that one of his earliest memories is of sitting on his grandfather's shoulders proudly watching the Apollo astronauts return to Hawaii after their splashdown in the Pacific. But in *Dreams*, even this event is an occasion for outrage, as Obama asks: "How could America send men into space and still keep its black citizens in bondage?"

American affluence offends Obama. The vast upper-middle class lives in a land of isolation and sterility. As a teenager, he envies the white homes in the suburbs but senses that the big pretty houses contain "quiet depression" and "loneliness," represented by "a mother sneaking a tumbler of gin in the afternoon." American consumer culture is comforting but mentally and spiritually numbing, yielding a "long hibernation."

Studying U.S. law at Harvard, Obama concludes it is mainly about "expediency or greed." Working in a large modern corporation, he sees himself as a "spy behind enemy lines." Even science and technology draw his disdain as he warns of "technology that spits out goods from its robot mouth."

Finishing *Dreams*, I could not recall a single positive sentence about the United States or European society. I reread the book specifically looking for positive remarks. The pickings were lean. Obama does write glowingly of JFK's Camelot and its promise of a "bright new world," but concludes this promise was a mere illusion quickly transformed into "war, riot, and famine." At the end of the book, Obama acknowledges that "faith in other people" can be found everywhere: among Christians as well as Muslims and in Kansas as well as his beloved Kenya. If you're looking for rousing patriotism, that's about as good as Obama gets.

Earlier this year, Michelle Obama made headlines by declaring that her husband's primary victories were the first time she had ever been "proud of my country." Michelle's remark simply echoes the assessment Barack presents in his 442-page autobiography: Aside from a few comments about what he regards as the largely unsuccessful struggle for civil rights in the Sixties, Obama has nothing positive to say about his country. Even his hopes for the future are modest and "sometimes hard to sustain."

POST-RACIAL OBAMA

Obama is touted as a post-racial statesman who sees beyond the narrow issue of white versus black. The Obama of his autobiography is, to the contrary, obsessed with race: Almost all of *Dreams* is about race and race conflict.

Obama's early life is marked by uncertainty and rootlessness. Born in Hawaii, he is abandoned by his black Kenyan father at age two. At six he goes to live in Indonesia with his white mother and Indonesian stepfather. At age ten, he leaves his mother and returns to Hawaii, where he spends the rest of his youth, living mainly with his lower-middle-class white grandparents and attending an expensive, almost-all-white prep school.

In multiracial Hawaii, Obama's encounters with racism, he admits, are pretty slight. On occasion, he deploys what he calls a "bad-assed nigger pose," but he understands its artificiality. Obama seems well accepted by the youth around him, but, inside, he feels anxious and apart. A turning point in the narrative occurs when some of his white teenage friends attend an otherwise all-black party with him but feel uncomfortable and ask to leave. Obama is enraged and wants to punch his friends.

He begins to inundate himself in black literature: Richard Wright, Ralph Ellison, James Baldwin, and W. E. B. DuBois. Saturated with themes of anger and alienation, Obama withdraws into a "smaller and smaller coil of rage." He suffers a "nightmare vision" of black powerlessness and feels whites have maimed blacks with a tragic "self contempt." Malcolm X becomes his favorite author, although he admits all the talk about "blue-eyed devils and apocalypse" is a bit much.

Teenage Obama now sees himself as a "would-be black." He begins to deliberately craft a black identity with alienation and anger at its foundation. The reader of *Dreams* cannot help being struck by the unexplained contrast between the circumstances of Obama's life—an opportunity to attend a fine school, white grandparents who love him—and his great anger at white society.

Today, Candidate Obama presents himself as a multiracial American who is proud of his mixed ancestry and can comfortably draw from both his white and his black roots. In *Dreams*, he takes the opposite stance. He deliberately and repeatedly rejects a multiracial identity. For example, attending an expensive private college in California, he meets many young people of mixed black and white ancestry who view themselves, not as black, but as multiracial. Obama specifically rejects this option as a sellout. He also rejects integration as a goal because it is "a one-way street. The minority is assimilated into the dominant culture, not the other way around."

After college, Obama has an affluent white girlfriend who loves and wants to marry him. She brings him to visit her family, who warmly accept him. Obama is attached to the girl and respects the family's deep cultural heritage, but he eventually dumps her because she is not black. He feels that if he marries her he will ultimately be assimilated into a foreign white culture, a fate that is unacceptable to him.

Obama comes to define and identify himself as a black man. As a young man he views his white ancestry not as an asset, but as an impediment to achieving authentic blackness. The dozens of cultural and historic figures appearing throughout *Dreams* are almost all black. (White author Joseph Conrad makes a token appearance as a deranged racist.) Obama identifies his principal role models: Malcolm X, Nelson Mandela, Martin Luther King, and W. E. B. DuBois. He states that while he might love his white grandfather and Indonesian stepfather, he could "never emulate" them because of the racial difference: They were "white men and brown men whose fates didn't speak to my own."

Obama is fascinated by his black ancestry. When he journeys to Kenya he has a deep sense of joy and belonging—he feels he has finally come home. By contrast, he has very little interest in his white ancestors or in the history of white America. He views U.S. history simply as a melodrama in which whites crush blacks (although class oppression and brutality against other minorities provide secondary plotlines).

It is true that Obama never abandons his affection for his white mother and grandparents. The memory of his immediate white relatives does remind him that not all whites are culpable racists and that some "could be exempted from the general category of distrust." But beyond this he has no identification or psychic ties to larger white society.

Dreams does present one exception to Obama's black exclusiveness. As Obama studies radical Marxist-Leninist literature (Frantz Fanon, neocolonialism, etc.), he comes to see himself as the champion not just of blacks but of the downtrodden of all races. But this shift only distances him farther from the dominant white and European culture, which he views as the focal point of global exploitation. Even in his thirties, he writes with enthusiasm about the Viet Cong, the Mau Mau Uprising, and black rioters in Detroit who lashed out with "street crime and revolution" against complacent white oppressors.

HATRED

Generally, Obama sees an unbridgeable gulf between races: "The other race would always remain just that: menacing, alien, and apart." He states that at the core of black consciousness is the experience of white hatred of blacks. This hatred inspires an anger in turn that can either be directed out toward whites or in toward blacks themselves, in self-loathing:

[Black awareness] hadn't arisen simply from struggles with pestilence or drought, or even mere poverty. [It] had arisen out of a very particular experience with hate [of whites toward blacks]. That hate hadn't gone away; it formed a counternarrative buried deep within each person and at the center of which stood white people—some cruel, some ignorant, sometimes a single face, sometimes just a faceless image of a system claiming power over our lives.

As a youth, Obama is shocked when a black mentor tells him that "black people have reason to hate," but later comes to accept this view. He ponders whether the "ghostly figure" of white hatred can ever be "exorcised" from black dreams. And he goes so far as to ask whether blacks can love themselves without hating whites, but provides no answer.

Candidate Obama declared that he was shocked when he heard Rev. Jeremiah's Wright's outrageous remarks about American society. Despite the fact that he had been a member of Wright's church for over a decade, Obama asserted that he had never heard such remarks from his spiritual mentor before.

But in the autobiography, Wright's rants are in plain view. It is obvious that Obama is drawn to Wright's ministry not in ignorance, but precisely because of the Reverend's politics. In *Dreams*, Wright asserts: "Life's not safe for a black man in this country, Barack. Never has been. Probably never will be." Obama apparently agrees, ignoring the obvious facts that nearly all black homicides are committed by other blacks, and that the number of violent crimes committed by blacks against whites is about eight times greater than the number of such crimes by whites against blacks.

When Wright, in the pages of *Dreams*, rants from the pulpit about Hiroshima and proclaims that "white folks' greed runs a world in need," it's not so jarring, since Obama has been saying pretty much the same thing throughout the book. Obama expresses joy and a real sense of belonging in connection with only three places: his childhood home in Indonesia, Kenya, and in the pews of Reverend Wright's Trinity United Church.

OBAMA AND THE UNDERCLASS

In his personal life, Obama has received highly favorable treatment from white society. His grievance appears, at least on the surface, to be abstract rather than personal. It is the existence of the black poor and underclass that justifies his alienation from and hostility to his nation. For Obama, the black ghetto epitomizes the callousness, greed, and injustice of U.S. society.

Obama became a community organizer in south Chicago to save the black urban poor and underclass. This was no mere job to Obama; it was a quasi-religious calling, his mission in life, offering the promise of personal "redemption." But at only one point does Obama pause in his narrative and ask the big questions. Contemplating the tangle of homicide, drug addiction, alcoholism, out-of-wedlock childbearing, and educational failure that blights the public-housing complex where he is working, he asks: What causes this? Who is responsible? After all, there are no white people there, "no cigar-chomping crackers . . . no club-wielding Pinkerton thugs."

With this question, Obama broaches the central paradox of modern race relations. Why, at a point when white society ended segregation, created affirmative action, and erected a massive new welfare state, did the self-destructive behaviors of the black lower classes soar, and entire communities begin spiraling downward in devastating social entropy? But, having raised this question, Obama offers no answer. The only solution he suggests is increased HUD funding. Some pages later he returns to vague charges about racism and hidden structures of power.

Elsewhere in *Dreams*, however, Obama hints at an explanation for this silence. He says that focusing on the self-destructive behavior of the black underclass smacks of "the explanations that whites had always offered of black poverty: that we continued to suffer from, if not genetic inferiority, then cultural weakness." A focus on behavior will only confirm the "worst suspicions" of blacks about themselves, pushing them deeper into helplessness and despair.

Black well-being therefore requires that the blame for black behavior always be placed in historic context—that is, shifted to whites. If 69 percent of black children are born out of wedlock, if blacks kill blacks, if black-run schools don't teach, it is the white man's fault. Alternative explanations will only relieve white guilt while raising black self-doubt.

SELF-PORTRAIT OF THE AUTHOR

Dreams from My Father reveals Barack Obama as a self-constructed, racially obsessed man who regards most whites as oppressors. It is the work of a clever but shallow thinker who confuses ideological cliché for insight — a man who sees U.S. history as a narrow, bitter tale of race and class victimization. The Barack Obama presented in these pages is not electable to national office. No wonder that Obama, aided by a compliant media, has created a new self for public view, one the Obama of *Dreams* wouldn't recognize and probably would disdain.

September 1, 2008

Soldier for Stronger

The candidate of change helped keep Chicago politics dirty

By David Freddoso

What is it like to work for the government of Cook County, Ill.? Simple. If you have the right political connections, you get the job. You get the raise. You get the promotion. You don't need to be qualified. You might not even need an interview. The job might not even be advertised to the public.

If you don't have the political connections, you might get a job, but you don't get the raise. You get no promotions, but you do get plenty of extra work that falls outside your job description. At some point, you're probably assigned to train an unqualified political stooge, sent from "downtown" to take that supervisory job for which you applied and for which you were actually qualified.

This system has a clear purpose. It is the basic building block of a political machine. It allows politicians to maintain a standing army of pamphleteers, door-knockers, fundraisers, and campaign contributors at taxpayer expense. Such an army can make the difference in a close election. More important, it deters serious political opponents from even trying.

This is how the late John Stroger, former president of the Cook County Board of Commissioners, allegedly kept himself in power until a stroke forced him to retire in 2006. Nothing has changed under his successor—his son, Todd Stroger—according to a 54-page federal report featuring numerous quotes from government employees' complaints. Cook County's federal compliance administrator, former circuit-court judge Julia Nowicki, received 240 such complaints in the first year following her court appointment to oversee county employment practices.

There's no reason the Stroger machine should still be in power. Not long ago, true reformers from both parties worked to bring it down in two different elections, and with Barack Obama's help might have succeeded either time. Instead, Obama ignored the effort in the primary election, and endorsed the machine candidate in the general.

MACHINE POLITICS

Nowicki's February 2008 report includes the charming story of one politically connected employee who just couldn't contain his excitement:

> On his first day in the department, he told a number of his new co-workers he was a "Soldier for Stroger" and he was going to become their supervisor. . . . One witness claims after working at the department for a total of five hours, the employee had already identified co-workers he intended to impose severe discipline upon when he became supervisor.

Sure enough, this individual *was* promoted to supervisor. Nowicki included dozens of similar complaints—Cook County employees' being pressured into political activities and being denied promotions when they refused. She speculated that more employees would come forward but for their fear of retaliation from the young Todd Stroger and his political allies, who took over in late 2006. She wrote that Todd Stroger's human-resources staff appeared to keep multiple personnel files in order to "cover" patronage employment. Stroger denounced Nowicki's report, but admitted later that he had not read it.

It's clear that, in this case, machine politics worked the way they were meant to. John Stroger faced only token opposition for a decade following his 1994 election. And the nonpartisan, Chicago-based Better Government Association provides the following numbers:

- Between early 1999 and the middle of 2005, Stroger raised approximately $2,413,246 in itemized contributions.
- At least $615,078.99 (25.5 percent) came from county contractors and their owners, agents, and employees.
- At least $624,543 (25.8 percent) came from Cook County employees who ultimately report to his office.

More than half of John Stroger's campaign cash was coming from people whose pockets he was lining with tax dollars. And with tax dollars serving him so well, it's no wonder Stroger liked high taxes. In his final two years in office alone, he endorsed a 2 percent hotel-motel tax, a 2 percent "prepared food and beverage" tax, a $200 "automatic amusement device" tax, increases of 8.5 percent and $1 per pack in the property and cigarette taxes respectively, and a tripling of court fees from $5 to $15. He also helped create "tax districts" to assess various special-purpose taxes.

His son Todd has kept the business going. He rammed a sales-tax increase through the Cook County Board of Commissioners; the hike went into effect in early July, and it gives Chicago the highest sales-tax rate of any major city in the United States (10.25 percent).

The younger Stroger often makes no attempt to hide hirings that most would find suspicious. Immediately upon inheriting his father's office, he promoted his cousin to county CFO and gave her a 12 percent pay hike the following month. He hired a friend's wife and a childhood friend to six-figure jobs. He hired an unqualified friend to a top health job—created just for this friend, apparently. When the newspapers discovered this last hire, the friend got demoted to a position that pays a mere $86,000 a year.

While handing out salaries to his buddies, Todd Stroger claimed the county lacked funds. He shut down several health clinics, laid off hundreds of nurses from the county hospital named after his father, and cut 43 prosecutors from the state attorney's office. In total, 1,700 county workers were laid off. Few, presumably, were "Soldiers for Stroger."

MARCH 2006: OBAMA'S SILENCE

As a presidential candidate, Obama has styled himself a reformer. But in early 2006 he knew exactly how the Stroger machine worked, was the most popular politician in Illinois, and had already become a star in the national Democratic party. Were there any link between style and substance—had Obama lifted even his pinkie finger in the name of a county government "we can believe in"—there would be no Stroger in power today. The problem is, had he endorsed the elder Stroger's serious challenger in the March 2006 Democratic primary, he might have lost the support of some of his most important allies and donors.

That reformist challenger, Forrest Claypool, was a progressive county commissioner. Local politicians of the Left and the Right, weary of corruption, lined up behind Claypool in the kind of post-partisanship Obama extols today. The other anti-Stroger candidate, Democratic commissioner Michael Quigley, dropped out of the race to present a unified reform campaign—he even became Claypool's campaign manager. He declared that Stroger "cynically abuses" the trust of poor people who depend on county government, by "wasting precious resources on the hangers-on—the contractors and the patronage workers."

Media outlets of all stripes joined in. The *Chicago Tribune* editorialized that "county government works for Stroger's pals, not for the people and businesses that pay taxes. And it certainly doesn't work for the impoverished people who have nowhere else to turn." Days before the primary election, *Chicago Sun-Times* columnist Neil Steinberg framed the voters' choice this way:

> Isn't it enough that Stroger has turned Cook County government into a bog of waste, cronyism and incompetence? Isn't it enough that a solid, respectable, smart alternative exists? Claypool is a longtime reformer who has fought heroically to make Cook County better and more effective—if you are voting to try to improve the vital Cook County services, the vote is for Claypool. If you vote your race [Stroger was black], for any clown, no matter how ignored and betrayed you are year in, year-out, then go for Stroger.

In the last two weeks, it appeared that Claypool might pull off a victory. But Stroger pulled out all the stops, with Chicago mayor Richard M. Daley and even Bill Clinton recording ads on his behalf. The machine organizations worked overtime to turn out the pro-Stroger vote.

Stroger won by seven percentage points—42,000 of 600,000 votes cast. Black voters carried Stroger, which is why it's so important that Claypool's supporters didn't include Barack Obama: By withholding his endorsement, Obama probably saved the machine.

It is no mystery why he did so. A Claypool endorsement would have alienated Emil Jones Jr., the machine politician who claims, not inaccurately, to have "made" Obama a U.S. senator in the 2004 election. It would have angered Mayor Daley, who controls Chicago's political money (and whose machine puts Stroger's to shame). It might have upset Obama's close friend Tony Rezko—who had given Stroger nearly $150,000, who once served as Stroger's finance chairman, and who had business ties to the Stroger family. It would have slighted every alderman, county commissioner, and ward boss who had door-knockers and small donors and family members on the county payroll.

Claypool has been a good sport about his loss, and now supports Obama's presidential campaign. But earlier this year, he became a bit despondent when asked why Obama had failed to help him in 2006. "I don't know," he told television journalist Jeff Berkowitz. "I mean, look, politics is complex. People have multiple relationships and they do the things they have to do and believe in."

Barack Obama has never done or even said anything to help solve Chicago's problem. He cannot do so because he has "multiple relationships"; his political allies—not just the Strogers, but nearly all of the politicians upon whom he depends for support—*are* Chicago's problem.

NOVEMBER 2006: LIES AND SCARE TACTICS

There was still a chance, in the general election, to defeat the Strogers. But instead of keeping silent as he had in the primaries, Obama supported the machine.

The elder Stroger, who suffered his stroke just before winning the primary election, disappeared from public view for three full months. He would eventually drop off the ballot, but not before the June 26 deadline for independent candidates to file. That way, he could execute a bait-and-switch without letting the ensuing controversy create an opening for a credible third-party opponent. John Stroger would exit the race, and the friendly Cook County Democratic party would choose his son Todd to take his place. Reform-minded Democrats—including U.S. Rep. Danny Davis—tried to prevent this shady electoral stunt, but to no avail. The fix was in.

Progressive Chicagoans were not happy with this outcome. Conservatives were fuming. Todd Stroger was an underachieving alderman, criticized by one liberal columnist as an "unimaginative legislative drone." Claypool said he would not vote for Todd Stroger. Several

Democrats—including Frank Coconate, chairman of the Northwest Side Democratic Organization—went so far as to endorse the Republican candidate (former Democrat Tony Peraica).

The press actually thought Peraica had a chance, even though Cook County had not had a Republican board president in 36 years. Once again, liberals and conservatives came together, this time behind a Republican. But Obama endorsed the young Stroger in a widely publicized letter to supporters, co-signed by Illinois's senior senator, Dick Durbin. They wrote:

> Today we write to urge your attention to one race in particular. Our friend, Todd Stroger, former state representative and alderman, is candidate for president of the Cook County Board. Please consider voting for Todd. . . . Todd is a good progressive Democrat, who will bring those values and sensibilities to the job.

The endorsement disgusted Chicago liberals. *Chicago Tribune* commentator Eric Zorn wrote of it:

> Obama and Durbin take an epistolary dive into the mud and start yammering in the letter about Republican challenger Tony Peraica's conservative stance on social issues that almost never come before the County Board. In particular, they raise the fear that Peraica would unilaterally put a halt to abortions at county hospitals, even though Peraica has repeatedly pledged that he will not.

"We've come too far for that," says the letter.

And Obama has come too far as an inspiring new breed of politician on the national scene to muck around in local politics, endorsing machine hack candidates and substituting party for principle. Or so you'd imagine.

Welcome to the "new politics." Obama put partisanship ahead of reform, using what both liberals and conservatives recognized as lies and scare tactics. Stroger defeated his opponent in an unusually close general election in November 2006.

Todd Stroger is not the only questionable candidate Obama has endorsed. In the same primary election in which he failed to endorse Forrest Claypool, Obama supported a candidate for state treasurer who, through his family bank, had been personally involved in loans to organized-crime figures—and who misled the press when first asked about it. The following year, Obama would endorse an alderman who once allegedly pulled a gun on her colleagues during a contentious ward-redistricting hearing. (The former candidate won, the latter lost.)

In 2007, Obama endorsed Mayor Daley for reelection—barely two months after three of Daley's top aides received federal prison sentences for fraud in connection with running the City Hall patronage machine, and barely a year after dozens of city contractors and employees had been convicted of trading city contracts for campaign contributions and bribes. These included high-ranking Daley aides and appointees.

Barack Obama's efforts to preserve the Windy City's crooked machine politics are typical of the approach he has taken toward reform throughout his service in both Springfield and Washington. He talks of change, but he simultaneously uses the existing corrupt system to get ahead. It is a far cry from the message that has so impressed his supporters.

September 1, 2008

Meandering Toward Disaster

The perils of making a left-wing ideologue Commander-in-Chief

By Andrew C. McCarthy

On the War on Terror, as with most issues, it can be difficult to understand Barack Obama's thinking if you listen only to his finely wrought speeches. But if you take the time to watch as Obama meanders toward a position, understanding him is easy.

Case in point: the Supreme Court's abysmal *Boumediene* decision in June, extending the constitutional right of habeas corpus (the right to have one's detention reviewed by a court) to alien enemy combatants held by the military at Guantanamo Bay. Obama was heartened by the ruling. As is his wont upon straying from the TelePrompTer, he dug himself a hole, this time in the form of an impromptu paean to pre-9/11 days, when terrorism was managed as though it were a garden-variety law-enforcement matter. "What we know," he proclaimed on June 16, "is that, in previous terrorist attacks—for example, the first attack against the World Trade Center—we were able to arrest those responsible, put them on trial. They are currently in U.S. prisons, incapacitated."

What we actually know is that everything Obama said was wrong.

We were not able to arrest all of those responsible even for the 1993 WTC bombing—one of the plotters escaped and was harbored for a decade by Saddam Hussein's Iraq (you remember, the place where Obama says there were no terrorists until the U.S. invasion). Of the two dozen terrorists indicted for al-Qaeda's 1998 American-embassy bombings, which killed more than 200 people, only five have been prosecuted. That number does not include Mamdouh Mahmud Salim, al-Qaeda founder who was not tried for his role in the attacks because he exploited the relatively weak security of the civilian criminal-justice system to attempt an escape during a meeting with his lawyers, maiming a prison guard in the process; he was consequently sentenced to 32 years in prison for attempted murder. The Clinton administration did not even bother to file indictments for the attacks on Khobar Towers (19 U.S. airmen killed) and the USS *Cole* (17 U.S. sailors killed). And the fugitive Osama bin Laden was not exactly incapacitated by his grand-jury indictment in June 1998—he orchestrated the embassy bombings, the *Cole* bombing, and 9/11 from Afghanistan, where the FBI has not had much success executing arrest warrants.

The McCain camp pounced on Obama's gaffe, sending him into his familiar back-pedal dance. As usual, Obama argued that the real problem was that Republican fear-mongers and benighted commentators were failing to grasp the elegant nuance of his thinking. (After all, he has taught constitutional law in an elite law school!) Obama said he had simply praised the pre-9/11 enforcement strategy and gone on to fault Bush for abandoning it. Why on earth would anyone think he was *endorsing* what he had praised? Obama insisted he had merely meant "that we can abide by due process and abide by basic concepts of rule of law and still crack down on terrorists." Meaning . . . what? Civilian trials for everyone? Obama wouldn't say, but he wanted at least habeas corpus for everyone: "The question is whether or not, as the Supreme Court said, people who are being held have a chance to at least suggest that 'Hey, you've got the wrong guy,' or 'I shouldn't be here.' It's not a question about whether or not they're free." Got that?

Richard Clarke thought he had it. The former Clinton counterterrorism czar and Obama adviser told ABC News that even Osama bin Laden should have the habeas corpus "right to go to federal court and ask the government to release him." Clarke's assessment was not only in sync with Obama's Delphic circumlocutions but was also an entirely accurate statement of what *Boumediene* holds. And that is precisely the problem: Obama's script calls for him to favor the Supreme Court's ruling, which is wildly popular with the Left, but to do so only by dilating on "due process" and "the rule of law"—lest the fog lift and voters grasp that Obama's idea of "cracking down on terrorists" includes conferring American civil rights upon Osama bin Laden.

That is why, in a press gaggle on June 18, Obama declined to "speculate" on how, if president, he would handle bin Laden, were al-Qaeda's emir to be captured. Gone, though, was the candidate's enthusiasm for trials in the criminal-justice system, which had been in evidence just two days before. The important things, Obama now stressed, were that bin Laden not be turned into a "martyr," and that he be handled "in a way that allows the entire world to understand the murderous acts that he's engaged in." Given that bin Laden himself has both declared war on the United States and claimed credit for sundry mass-murder attacks, one wonders what exactly it is that Obama thinks "the entire world" is in the dark about.

Having dealt with that question, Obama floated another trial balloon: an international tribunal on the Nuremberg model. "One of the hallmarks, one of the high-water points, I think, of U.S. foreign policy," said he, "was the Nuremberg trials. Because the world had not seen before victors behave in ways that advanced a set of universal principles. And that set a tone for post-war reconstruction and creation of an international order that I think was extraordinarily important." But what were these universal principles? At Nuremberg, there was no appellate process, no habeas corpus, and no access to American civilian courts to say, "Hey, you've got the wrong guy." For several of the defendants, the tribunals were followed in short order by a date with the business end of a noose.

In contrast, the military commissions ordered by President Bush and authorized by Congress provide lavish procedural protections for enemy combatants charged with war crimes: In addition to taxpayer-funded counsel, the presumption of innocence, the ability to call witnesses and introduce evidence, sentencing protocols, and the like, the law prescribes military appeals and adds systematic access to the civilian justice system for review by the D.C. Circuit Court of Appeals and, finally, the Supreme Court. To note that the World War II tribunals did not come close to this quantum of due process would be gross understatement. Yet Obama, admirer of a Nuremberg process whose authors would not for a moment have brooked such a breathtaking judicial excess as *Boumediene*, staunchly opposed the Military Commissions Act.

When Obama does take an unwavering position, it is to weaken executive war powers. Most of the time, though, he shifts incrementally from this default setting, nudged by the calculation of the moment. His dizzying three-day metamorphosis from Clinton-style enforcement to habeas corpus to Nuremberg is not singular. In early 2006, he opposed reauthorization of the Patriot Act (passed in 2001, before he was in the Senate) because it gave government "powers it didn't need to invade our privacy without cause or suspicion." But when opposition became politically untenable, he got on board—protesting that intervening civil liberties "improvements" justified his switch.

While neck-and-neck with Hillary Clinton in the later primaries, Obama planted himself firmly in the fringe, opposing a surveillance-reform bill that had garnered overwhelming bipartisan support in the Democrat-controlled Congress. The reform was desperately needed to reverse a court ruling that had imperiled the CIA and NSA's authority to gather intelligence abroad. Sensible Democrats understood that they could not afford to block intelligence collection and vest al-Qaeda with Fourth Amendment rights. But the bill was at odds with a hard-Left cause célèbre: denying legal immunity to the telecommunications companies that assisted the Bush administration's post-9/11 monitoring of cross-border communications. Obama not only voted with the fringe, he promised to filibuster any immunity bill. But by the time the final vote came up in July, he had the nomination sewn up. *Filibuster? Surely you jest.* As flip follows flop, he voted yea—immunity and all.

At bottom, Obama is a calculating left-wing ideologue, and that is how he would govern when it comes to the war—and much else. His unvarying first instinct is that the pursuit of America's interests overseas, especially their pursuit by the use of military force, is imperial and provocative. That pursuit, and not fundamentalist Islam's propensity to spawn violent radicalism, is for him the real threat. At home, Obama sees sensible measures to protect the country from attack as violations of civil liberties and a slippery slope to "profiling"—a revealing reminder of the race-conscious, criminal-friendly activism that marked Obama's years as a Chicago "community organizer" and an Illinois legislator.

Though often surprisingly uninformed, Obama is shrewd, so he is willing to soft-pedal and even abandon his principles to court voters who do not share them. But even if Obama must deflect attention from those principles, he is constantly pursuing them, in Fabian fashion and under the guise of such euphemisms as "social justice," "due process," "rule of law," and, of course, "America's reputation in the world."

On the war, an Obama administration would give Americans more than our reputation to worry about.

September 1, 2008

Senator Stealth

How to advance radical causes when no one's looking

By Stanley Kurtz

A fter hearing about Barack Obama's ties to the Rev. Jeremiah Wright, Bill Ayers, Bernardine Dohrn, Fr. Michael Pfleger, and the militant activists of ACORN (the Association of Community Organizations for Reform Now), it should be clear to everyone that his extremist roots run deep. But the presumptive Democratic presidential nominee has yet another connection with the world of far-Left radicalism. Obama has long been linked—through foundation grants, shared political activism, collaboration on legislation and tactics, and mutual praise and support—with the Chicago-based Gamaliel Foundation, one of the least known yet most influential national umbrella groups for church-based "community organizers."

The same separatist, anti-American theology of liberation that was so boldly and bitterly proclaimed by Obama's pastor is shared, if more quietly, by Obama's Gamaliel colleagues. The operative word here is "quietly." Gamaliel specializes in ideological stealth, and Obama, a master student of Gamaliel strategy, shows disturbing signs of being a sub rosa radical himself. Obama's legislative tactics, as well as his persistent professions of non-ideological pragmatism, appear to be inspired by his radical mentors' most sophisticated tactics. Not only has Obama studied, taught, and apparently absorbed stealth techniques from radical groups like Gamaliel and ACORN, but in his position as a board member of Chicago's supposedly nonpartisan Woods Fund, he quietly funneled money to his radical allies—at the very moment he most needed their support to boost his political career. It's high time for these shadowy, perhaps improper, ties to receive a dose of sunlight.

The connections are numerous. Gregory Galluzzo, Gamaliel's co-founder and executive director, served as a trainer and mentor during Obama's mid-1980s organizing days in Chicago. The Developing Communities Project, which first hired Obama, is part of the Gamaliel network. Obama became a consultant and eventually a trainer of community organizers for Gamaliel. (He also served as a trainer for ACORN.) And he has kept up his ties with Gamaliel during his time in the U.S. Senate.

The Gamaliel connection appears to supply a solution to the riddle of Obama's mysterious political persona. On one hand, he likes to highlight his days as a community organizer—a profession with proudly radical roots in the teachings of Chicago's Saul Alinsky, author of the highly influential text *Rules for Radicals*. Obama even goes so far as to make the community-organizer image a metaphor for his distinctive conception of elective office. On the other hand, Obama presents himself as a post-ideological, consensus-minded politician who favors pragmatic, common-sense solutions to the issues of the day. How can Obama be radical and post-radical at the same time? Perhaps by deploying Gamaliel techniques. Gamaliel organizers have discovered a way to fuse their Left-extremist political beliefs with a smooth, non-ideological surface of down-to-earth pragmatism: the substance of Jeremiah Wright with the appearance of Norman Vincent Peale. Could this be Obama's secret?

FROM REVELATION TO REVOLUTION

Before outlining Gamaliel's techniques of political stealth, we need to identify the views that they are camouflaging. These can be found in Dennis Jacobsen's book *Doing Justice: Congregations and Community Organizing*. Jacobsen is the pastor of Incarnation Lutheran Church in Milwaukee and director of the Gamaliel National Clergy Caucus. Jacobsen's book, which is part of the first-year reading list for new Gamaliel organizers, lays out the underlying theology of Gamaliel's activities. While Jacobsen's book was published in 2001, it is based on presentations Jacobsen has been making at Gamaliel's clergy-training center since 1992 and clearly has Galluzzo's endorsement. So while we cannot be sure that Obama has read or taught *Doing Justice*, the book certainly embodies a political perspective to which Obama's more than

20 years of friendship with Galluzzo, and his stint as a Gamaliel instruc-
tor, would surely have exposed him.

In Jacobsen's conception, America is a sinful and fallen nation
whose pervasive classism, racism, and militarism authentic Christians
must constantly resist. Drawing on the Book of Revelation, Jacobsen
exhorts, "Fallen, fallen is Babylon the great! . . . Come out of her, my
people, so that you do not take part in her sins." The United States,
Jacobsen maintains, employs nationalism, propaganda, racism, bogus
"civil religion," and class enmity to bolster its entrenched and oppressive
corporate system. Authentic Christians forced to live in such a nation can
"come out of Babylon," says Jacobsen, only by entering into "a perpetual state of internal exile."

Of course, many believers do feel at home in the United States, but
according to Jacobsen, these inauthentic and misguided Christians have
been lulled into the false belief that the United States is somehow different from other countries—that it stands as a genuine defender of freedom
and democracy. According to Jacobsen, the desire of most Americans to
create a safe, secure life for themselves and their families constitutes an
unacceptable emotional distancing from the sufferings of the urban poor.
Jacobsen says that whenever he feels himself seduced by the American
dream of personal security—this "unconscionable removal from the
lives of those who suffer"—he rejects its pull as the deplorable
"encroachment of America on my soul." To "feel at home in the United
States," maintains Jacobsen, is not only to fall victim to a scarcely disguised form of political despotism; it is to betray Christianity itself.

Although Jacobsen acknowledges that the sufferings of the poor in
America do not quite rise to the level of the Nazi Holocaust, he nonetheless finds a similarity: "The accommodation and silence of the church
amidst Nazi atrocities are paralleled by the accommodation and silence
of the church in this country amidst a calculated war against the poor."
He recounts being present at the Pentagon "to fast and vigil with a group
of religious resisters against the madness of nuclear build-up and militarism generated in that place" and is horrified when he sees that many
in the American military actually think of themselves as Christians. For
Jacobsen, this means that the church has "aligned itself with oppressive
forces and crucified its Lord anew."

Jacobsen has a low opinion of the food pantries, homeless shelters, and walk-a-thons that make up so much religious charitable activity in the United States. All that charity, says Jacobsen, tends to suppress the truth that the system itself is designed to benefit the prosperous and keep the poor down. He complains: "The Christians who are so generous with food baskets at Thanksgiving or with presents for the poor at Christmas often vote into office politicians whose policies ignore or crush those living in poverty." "Most churches do not operate on the basis of healthy agitation," he says, but instead "on the basis of manipulation, authoritarianism, or guilt-tripping."

The solution, says Jacobsen, is community organizing: "Metropolitan organizing offers a chance to end the warfare against the poor and to heal the divisions of class and race that separate this sick society." "Militant mass action . . . fueled by righteous anger," he maintains, offers authentic community, and therefore "the possibility of fulfillment in a vacuous society." He continues: "If the pain and human degradation all around us doesn't stir up within us sufficient anger to want to shake the foundations of this society, then it's probably best for us to go back to playing church."

Other than the sense of community that is generated by militant struggle, what does Jacobsen offer as the cure for America's ills? He is short on detail here, but there are tantalizing hints. Jacobsen invokes the communal property and absence of private ownership that prevailed among early Christians as a possible model. Despite his initial skepticism regarding such selflessness, says Jacobsen, he has seen this sort of "radical sharing of limited resources" on a trip to a poor African church in Tanzania. Unfortunately, says Jacobsen, "the church in the United States lacks community. The American church by and large is privatistic, insular, and individualistic. It reflects American culture."

These, then, are the beliefs at the spiritual heart of the Gamaliel Foundation's community-organizing efforts. They show clear echoes of Jeremiah Wright's and James Cone's black-liberation theology, and it's evident that Obama has an affinity for organizations that embody this point of view. But a question arises. Gamaliel's goal is to build church-based coalitions capable of wielding power on behalf of the poor. These congregation-based organizations are supposed to counterbalance and undercut America's oppressive power structures. Yet if most American Christians are deluded servants of a sinful and oppressive system, how can they be molded into a majority coalition for change? Given the privatistic, insular, and individualistic character of American culture, theological frankness might backfire and drive away potential allies, exactly as happened with Reverend Wright. Thus arises the need for stealth.

FAKE RIGHT, GO LEFT

It might have been all but impossible to penetrate the strategic thinking of Obama's cohorts if not for the fortuitous 2008 publication of *Organizing Urban America: Secular and Faith-based Progressive Movements*, by Rutgers political scientist Heidi Swarts. This is the first book-length study of the organizing tactics and political ideologies of Gamaliel and ACORN, the two groups to which Obama's community-organizing ties are closest. Swarts's study focuses on Gamaliel and ACORN in St. Louis, but given the degree of national coordination by both groups, the carry-over of her findings to Chicago is bound to be substantial. Because Swarts is highly sympathetic to the community-organizing groups she studies, she was granted an unusual degree of access to strategic discussions during her period of fieldwork.

Swarts calls groups like ACORN and (especially) Gamaliel "invisible actors," hidden from public view because they often prefer to downplay their efforts, because they work locally, and because scholars and journalists pay greater attention to movements with national profiles (like the Sierra Club or the Christian Coalition). Congregation-based community organizations like Gamaliel, by contrast, are often invisible even at the local level. A newspaper might report on a demonstration led by a local minister or priest, for example, without noticing that the clergyman in question is part of the Gamaliel network. "Though often hidden from view," says Swarts, "leaders have *intentionally* and *strategically* organized these movements that appear to well up and erupt from below."

Although Gamaliel and ACORN have significantly different tactics and styles, Swarts notes that their political goals and ideologies are broadly similar. Both groups press the state for economic redistribution. The tactics of Gamaliel and ACORN have been shaped in a "post-Alinsky" era of welfare reform and conservative resurgence, posing a severe challenge to those who wish to expand the welfare state. The answer these activists have hit upon, says Swarts, is to work incrementally in urban areas, while deliberately downplaying the far-Left ideology that stands behind their carefully targeted campaigns.

While ACORN's membership is fairly homogeneous, consisting chiefly of inner-city blacks and Hispanics, congregation-based community organizations like the Gamaliel Foundation tend to have more racially, culturally, and politically mixed constituencies. The need to overcome these divisions and gather a broad coalition behind its hard-Left agenda has pushed Gamaliel to develop what Swarts calls an "innovative cultural strategy." Because of the suspicions that blue-collar members might harbor toward its elite, liberal leaders, Gamaliel's main "ideological tactic," says Swarts, is to present its organizers as the opposite of radical, elite, or ideological. As Swarts explains, they deliberately refrain from using leftist jargon like "racism," "sexism," "classism," "homophobia," "oppression," or "multiple oppressions" in front of ordinary members— even though, amongst themselves, Gamaliel's organizers toss around this sort of lingo with abandon, just as Jacobsen does in his book.

Swarts supplies a chart listing "common working-class perceptions of liberal social movements" on one side, while displaying on the other side Gamaliel organizers' tricky tactics for getting around them. To avoid seeming like radicals or "hippies left over from the sixties," Gamaliel organizers are careful to wear conventional clothing and conduct themselves with dignity, even formality. Since liberal social movements tend to come off as naïve and idealistic, Gamaliel organizers make a point of presenting their ideas as practical, pragmatic, and down-to-earth. When no one else is listening, Gamaliel organizers may rail at "racism," "sexism," and "oppressive corporate systems," but when speaking to their blue-collar followers, they describe their plans as "common sense solutions for working families."

Although the Gamaliel agenda is deeply collectivist and redistributionist, organizers are schooled to frame their program in traditional American, individualist terms. As Swarts puts it:

> What makes [Gamaliel's] ideology liberal rather than
> conservative is that it advocates not private or voluntary solu-

tions but collective public programs. They seek action from the state: social welfare programs, redistribution, or regulation. . . . But publicly [Gamaliel and other congregation-based groups] usually emphasize individual responsibility on the part of authorities.

What Gamaliel really wants, in other words, is for the public as a whole to fork over funds to the government, but they're careful to frame this demand as a call for "personal responsibility" by particular government officials.

The relative homogeneity of ACORN's membership allows it to display its radicalism more openly. According to Swarts, ACORN members think of themselves as "oppositional outlaws" and "militants unafraid to confront the powers that be." Yet even ACORN has a deeper, hidden ideological dimension. "Long-term ACORN organizers . . . tend to see the organization as a solitary vanguard of principled leftists," says Swarts, while ordinary members rarely think in these overtly ideological terms; for them, it's more about attacking specific problems. In general, ACORN avoids programmatic statements. During a 1980 effort to purge conservatives from its ranks, however, the organization did release a detailed political platform—which Swarts calls "a veritable laundry list of progressive positions."

Although ACORN's radicalism is somewhat more frank than Gamaliel's, ACORN has an "innovative cultural strategy" of its own. ACORN's radicalism is incremental; it's happy to work toward ambitious long-term goals through a series of baby steps. For example, although ACORN has fought for "living wage" laws in several American cities, these affect only the small fraction of the workforce employed directly by city governments. The real purpose of ACORN's urban living-wage campaigns, says Swarts, is not economic but political. ACORN's long-term goal is an across-the-board minimum-wage increase at the state and federal levels. The public debate spurred by local campaigns is meant to prepare the political ground for ACORN's more ambitious political goals, and to build up membership in the meantime.

WITH A LITTLE HELP FROM MY FRIENDS
Throughout his career, Obama has drawn on all of these strategies. In

Illinois's Republican-controlled state senate, Obama specialized in incremental legislation, often drawn up in collaboration with groups like Gamaliel and ACORN. His tiny, targeted expansions of government-financed health care, for example, were designed to build political momentum for universal health care. And his claim to be a "common-sense pragmatist," rather than a leftist ideologue, comes straight out of the Gamaliel playbook.

New evidence now ties Obama still more closely to both organizations. Not only was Obama a trainer for Gamaliel and ACORN, he appears to have used his influence to secure a major increase in funding for both groups—arguably stretching the bounds of propriety in the process.

In 2005, the year after Obama was elected to the U.S. Senate, the Washington, D.C.–based Center for Community Change released a report titled "Promising Practices in Revenue Generation for Community Organizing." One of the report's authors was Jean Rudd, Obama's friend and the president of the Woods Fund during Obama's years on that foundation's board. Buried deep within the report lies the story of Obama's role in expanding the Woods Fund's financial support for groups like Gamaliel and ACORN.

Since the start of his organizing career, Obama was recognized by the Woods Fund as "a great analyst and interpreter of organizing," according to the 2005 report. Initially an adviser, Obama became a Woods Fund board member, and finally board chairman, serving as a key advocate of increased funding for organizing during that period. In 1995, the Woods Fund commissioned a special evaluation of its funding for community organizing—a report that eventually recommended a major expansion of financial support. Obama chaired a committee of organizers that advised the Woods Fund on this important shift.

The committee's report, "Evaluation of the Fund's Community Organizing Grant Program," is based on interviews with all the big names in Obama's personal organizer network. Greg Galluzzo and other Gamaliel Foundation officials were consulted, as were several ACORN organizers, including Madeline Talbott, Obama's key ACORN contact. Talbott, an expert on ACORN's tactics of confrontation and disruption, is quoted more often than any other organizer in the report, sometimes with additional comments from Obama himself. The report holds up Gamaliel and ACORN as models for other groups and supports Talbott's call for "'a massive infusion of resources' to make organizing a truly mass-based movement."

Support from the Woods Fund had importance for these groups that went way beyond the money itself. Since community organizers often use confrontation, intimidation, and "civil disobedience" in the service of their political goals, even liberal foundations sometimes find it difficult to fund them without risking public criticism. As the report puts it: "Some funders . . . are averse to confrontational tactics, and are loathe [sic] to support organizing for that reason. They essentially equate organizing with the embarrassment of their business and government associates." The Woods Fund is both highly respected and one of the few foundations to consistently support community organizing, so its money acts as a kind of Good Housekeeping Seal of Approval, providing political cover for other foundations interested in funding the hard Left. Obama apparently sought to capitalize on this effect, not only by expanding the Woods Fund's involvement in organizing, but by distributing the Woods report to a national network of potential funders.

Formally, the Woods Fund claims to be "non-ideological." According to the report: "This stance has enabled the Trustees to make grants to organizations that use confrontational tactics against the business and government 'establishments,' without undue risk of being criticized for partisanship." Yet ACORN received substantial funding from Woods, apparently aided by Obama's internal advocacy, and we now know that ACORN members have played key roles as volunteer ground troops in Obama's various political campaigns. That would seem to raise the specter of partisanship.

A 2004 article in *Social Policy* by Chicago ACORN leader Toni Foulkes, titled "Case Study: Chicago—The Barack Obama Campaign," explains that, given Obama's long and close relationship to ACORN, "it was natural for many of us to be active volunteers" in Obama's campaigns. Perhaps ACORN volunteers observed the technical legalities and helped Obama merely in their capacity as private citizens. Even so, it seems at least possible that Obama used his position at a supposedly nonpartisan foundation to direct money to an allegedly nonpartisan group, in pursuit of what were in fact nakedly partisan ends.

Given Obama's political aspirations, it's notable that the focus of his Woods Fund report is its call for "improving the tie between organizing and policy making" and shifting organizing's focus from local battles to "citywide or statewide coalitions." The report boldly criticizes Saul Alinsky himself for being excessively focused on local issues, complaining that "he did not seek to fundamentally upset the distribution of power in the wider society."

The ultimate goal of all these efforts—fundamental disruption of America's power structure, and economic redistribution along race, poverty, and gender lines—is entirely compatible with the program outlined by Dennis Jacobsen in *Doing Justice*. Obama could hardly have been unfamiliar with the general drift of Gamaliel ideology, especially given his reputation as an analyst of community organizing and his supervision of a comprehensive review of the field.

Even after becoming a U.S. senator, Obama has maintained his ties to the Gamaliel Foundation. According to an October 2007 report for the University of California by Todd Swanstrom and Brian Banks, "it is almost unheard of for a U.S. Senator to attend a public meeting of a community organization, but Senator Obama attended a Gamaliel affiliate public meeting in Chicago." Given this ongoing contact, given the radicalism of Gamaliel's core ideology, given Obama's close association with Gamaliel's co-founder, Gregory Galluzzo, given Obama's role as a Gamaliel consultant and trainer, and given Obama's outsized role in channeling allegedly "nonpartisan" funding to Gamaliel affiliates (and to his political ground troops at ACORN), some questions are in order. Obama needs to detail the nature of his ties to both Gamaliel and ACORN, and should discuss the extent of his knowledge of Gamaliel's guiding ideology. Ultimately, we need to know if Obama is the post-ideological pragmatist he sometimes claims to be, or in fact a stealth radical.

September 29, 2008

A Bad Dream

And one we've had before

By Jonah Goldberg

As the presidential race has been accelerating beyond the limits of Einsteinian physics, it's little wonder substantive commentary about Barack Obama's acceptance speech at the Democratic convention was so scarce. Of course, there was ample instant-punditry about the "spectacle" at Denver's Invesco Field—the Greek columns, the adoring throng of 80,000, and the historical poignancy of the speech's being given on the anniversary of Martin Luther King's "I Have a Dream" speech. But the next day John McCain picked Sarah Palin as his running mate; three days after that, the GOP convention commenced. Now Obama's address seems like it was a century ago.

And that's fitting. Because rather than a bold and visionary statement about the future—what some might expect from "The One"—the core theme of the speech was in fact very, very old.

Truth be told, most of it was merely dated. The Kerry-like and Gore-esque laundry list of programs and giveaways was standard Democratic fare. Indeed, as the *Dallas Morning News*'s Rod Dreher noted, whole passages were indistinguishable from similar speeches by Gore and Kerry in 2000 and 2004. This makes sense, because Barack Obama desperately wants to be indistinguishable from Gore and Kerry, because the pollsters say if he can convince voters he's a generic Democrat, he'll win. So, once again the Democratic nominee promises to be Santa Claus, bringing to mind Mencken's famous quip about Harry Truman's 1948 campaign: "If there had been any formidable body of cannibals in the country, he would have promised to provide them with free missionaries fattened at the taxpayers' expense."

But beneath the fresh coat of rhetorical paint on the calcified clichés of contemporary liberalism there is a deeper vision to Obama's speech, one that is both consistent with his rhetoric from the earliest days of his campaign and career and also perfectly in line with the ambitions of progressivism since its founding.

For generations politicians of both parties spoke about the "American dream," a phrase that, though ill-defined, usually conjures up some conception of the individual pursuit of happiness. To own your own home, care for your family, succeed in what you set out to do: This, for most people, is what the American dream is about. Whatever the American dream means to most Americans, it is emphatically not a collectivist concept (though the phrase was reportedly coined by the progressive historian James Truslow Adams, who did see it as a more collective ideal). For most of us, there is no one American dream, because my dream is different from your dream. Victory can be pursued by a group; happiness must be found alone.

The American dream, as most of us understand it, stands in marked contrast to the idea of the American promise, the central theme of Obama's speech and even of the Democratic convention as a whole. In 1909, *New Republic* founder Herbert Croly published his book *The Promise of American Life*, widely considered the bible of the progressive movement (a movement Obama has explicitly declared the precursor of his own campaign's mission). Felix Frankfurter dubbed the book "the most powerful single contribution to progressive thinking."

Unlike Obama, Croly did not have a wandering childhood abroad, but he was something of an internal exile. And he shared Obama's sense of being an outsider in America. Historian Eric Goldman wrote that Croly's fringe-intellectual, European-style upbringing led him to write about even his fellow progressives the "way foreign ambassadors talk about American baseball games." Something similar might be said of the man who mused that people who didn't vote for him were simply bitterly clinging to their sky god and boomsticks.

Obama and Croly also share a similar view of the intersection of religion and politics: They don't believe there is one, because the two things are identical. Croly embraced Christianity in college and later fell for Eastern spiritualism, but he never failed to see politics as an extension of religious messianism; Obama talks of using government to create a kingdom of heaven on earth. The black-liberation theology of

Obama's former church explicitly merges black-power politics and theological teaching to the point that one cannot discern one from the other. In *The Promise of American Life*, Croly yearned for a "national reformer . . . in the guise of St. Michael" and an "imitator of Christ" who would crush laissez-faire capitalism and cruel individualism. (Indeed, he wrote, an "individual has no meaning apart from the society in which his individuality has been formed.")

Croly is often described by his progressive fans as a heroic small-D democrat. But this is pure spin: Croly was a centralizer who despised the Jeffersonian tradition. He worshipped Lincoln for his centralizing power-politics and favored keeping big business as big as possible so as to make it a more effective tool of government. Indeed, what confuses many students of history is that he was a national-socialist (note the lower case, please) who used the word "democracy" as a rough substitute for what most would call socialism. "For better or worse," Croly proclaimed, "democracy cannot be disentangled from an aspiration toward human perfectibility." Even a cursory review of the *Federalist Papers* will reveal this wasn't the Founders' understanding of democracy. For Croly, the "promise" of America was the aim of replacing the American conception of "government" by the people with the European ideal of "the State" as the highest expression of "the people's" Rousseauian general will. He agreed wholeheartedly with Woodrow Wilson's and John Dewey's visions of a progressive America where every individual, in Wilson's words, "marr[ied] his interests to the State." Such a new America would come about through a national politico-religious "reconstruction."

Since the mid-1990s, Herbert Croly has enjoyed a fitful revival, particularly among self-described progressives desperate to find an intellectual lineage to the progressive era. Both Hillary Clinton and Barack Obama have explicitly claimed to be the incarnations of the original progressive spirit, though, out of either wisdom or ignorance, they refrain from spelling out what specific progressive ideas they find common cause with. (Presumably it wasn't the war-mongering, eugenics, racism, or disdain for civil liberties.)

Obama's acceptance speech in Denver was not expressly Crolyite, but those familiar with Croly's work can't help but hear the echoes. One can imagine that his real desire—if he hadn't been forced to make so much of it conventional boilerplate—was to offer a progressive Gettysburg Address, transforming the American dream into a strictly statist concept.

Obama's sleight of hand begins in the first paragraph. After he dispenses with the thank-yous, he says: "Four years ago, I stood before you and told you my story—of the brief union between a young man from Kenya and a young woman from Kansas who weren't well-off or well-known, but shared a belief that in America, their son could achieve whatever he put his mind to."

He continues in the next paragraph: "It is that promise that has always set this country apart—that through hard work and sacrifice, each of us can pursue our individual dreams but still come together as one American family, to ensure that the next generation can pursue their dreams as well. That's why I stand here tonight. Because for 232 years, at each moment when that promise was in jeopardy, ordinary men and women—students and soldiers, farmers and teachers, nurses and janitors—found the courage to keep it alive."

So far, it sounds as if Obama is simply going to use "American promise" as a stand-in for "American dream." After all, his version of the son-of-an-immigrant success story fits nicely within the idea of the American dream. But after the opening reference to "individual dreams," Obama's speech becomes a Deweyan alchemy spell to transmogrify individual liberty into collective action. The promise of America, for Obama, is the hope that one day we will live in a country where we all work together, where "one person's struggle is all of our struggles" (as he put it in his introductory video). The American promise, Obama insists, is "the idea that we are responsible for ourselves, but that we also rise or fall as one nation; the fundamental belief that I am my brother's keeper, I am my sister's keeper. That's the promise we need to keep. . . . Individual responsibility and mutual responsibility—that's the essence of America's promise."

It sounds benign, even noble, except for the central deceit in Obama's plea. The Biblical injunction to be your brother's keeper—what Obama calls "mutual responsibility"—is not a writ for government activism. You do not fulfill your obligation to look out for your fellow man by paying taxes, never mind by voting to impose them on others. Absent from Obama's rhetoric is any serious acknowledgment that there are countless mediating institutions between the individual and the state. Civil society—churches, schools, voluntary associations, etc.—provides the sinews of the mutual responsibility that exists outside of the sphere of government. But for Obama, as with Croly, it is all either/or: Either you're "on your own" or you're in the good hands of the all-state, and I'm not talking about an insurance company. This is a marked contrast with McCain's speech, which, in short, promised to reform government: Obama promises to reform *America* instead.

Obama does offer some concessions to the role entrepreneurialism plays in American society, but it's clear he sees business as an extension of politics. Businesses, he insists, "should live up to their responsibilities to create American jobs." Job creation is a wonderful thing, but it takes a community organizer's understanding of the private sector to think that it is the businessman's responsibility to create jobs. There are only two kinds of firms that go into business to create jobs: the ones that almost immediately go out of business and the ones that consider bilking taxpayers a noble endeavor.

Obama's disdain for the traditional notion of the American dream as the pursuit of happiness is palpable. "In Washington, they call this the Ownership Society, but what it really means is—you're on your own. Out of work? Tough luck. You're on your own. No health care? The market will fix it. You're on your own. Born into poverty? Pull yourself up by your own bootstraps—even if you don't have boots. You're on your own."

This philosophical myopia informs Obama's entire conception of politics. In his recent interview with Fox's Bill O'Reilly, Obama defended raising taxes on the wealthy on the grounds of "neighborliness": "If I am sitting pretty, and you've got a waitress who is making minimum wage plus tips, and I can afford it if she can't—what's the big deal for me to say, 'I'm going to pay a little bit more.' That is neighborliness." Perhaps that makes sense if you and your neighbors live in Hillary Clinton's village, but neighborliness by definition is not compulsory.

Obama's prism, however, isn't the Clintonite village, where everybody's business is everybody's business. Rather, his ideal for social organization is the Movement. "This too," he proclaimed in Denver, "is part of America's promise—the promise of a democracy where we can find the strength and grace to bridge divides and unite in common effort." It's telling how much Sarah Palin's and Rudy Giuliani's barbs at "community organizing" shook the Obama campaign. Hilariously, left-wing blogs shrieked that "Jesus was a community organizer, Pontius Pilate was a governor." Putting theological issues aside, whether or not Jesus could be called a community organizer, what's clear is that Obama isn't *that* kind of a community organizer. The comparison speaks volumes about a campaign that has been desperately trying to tamp down its perceived messianism. Let the record show that Jesus was not running for governor (and, as a colleague quipped, Pilate merely voted an Obama-like "present")—which is why Jesus, unlike Croly and Obama, didn't confuse Caesar's portfolio with God's.

At the end of his Invesco Field address, Obama returns to the speech he seems to have wanted to give. He notes that he's speaking on the 45th anniversary of Martin Luther King's "dream" speech. But it is not King's dream of colorblindness, in which individuals are respected regardless of color, that he invokes—but a different vision altogether. The message of King's speech is, according to Obama, that "in America, our destiny is inextricably linked, that together our dreams can be one." He continues, "'We cannot walk alone,' the preacher cried. 'And as we walk, we must make the pledge that we shall always march ahead. We cannot turn back.' . . . Not with so much work to be done; not with so many children to educate, and so many veterans to care for; not with an economy to fix, and cities to rebuild, and farms to save; not with so many families to protect and so many *lives to mend*. America, we cannot turn back. We cannot walk alone."

Perhaps not. But if we all end up walking toward a single dream, by definition it will not be the American dream, but Obama's.

November 3, 2008

Obama's Core

The West, for him, is not the best

By Michael Knox Beran

Leon Trotsky's *The Russian Revolution* does not occupy a high place in the literature of conservatism. But the old Bolshevik could on occasion be perceptive. Analyzing the improbable rise of Rasputin, he noted how frequently shamanism flourishes in the bowels of a decaying oligarchy, when the languishing elites crave the stimulus that only a certain kind of messianic figure can give. The commissar had a point. In the fourth *Eclogue*, Virgil beguiled the patricians of the collapsing Roman republic with a vision of a miraculous child who would inaugurate a golden age. Eighteen centuries later such charlatans as Mesmer and Cagliostro practiced their mystic arts in the salons of the *ancien régime*.

True to the morphology of exhausted elites, it is the privileged element in the American polity that has proved most susceptible to Barack Obama's appeal. Historians of the future, seeking to understand this enthusiasm, may well conclude that it was a kind of despair, the despair of those who, having lost their faith in the traditional remedial institutions of their culture, embraced a mirage.

T. S. Eliot put his finger on the problem when he compared the poetry of Dante to that of the modern age. Dante's poetry, Eliot said, stood for a "principle of order in the human soul, in society and in the universe." Eliot suggested that the old poetic culture of the West, with its emphasis on harmony, proportion, and order, brought coherence to the world and did much to reconcile men and women to the larger rhythms of life. The roots of this culture, Werner Jaeger showed in his classic study, *Paideia*, grew out of the Greek belief that poetry and music, together with rhythm and harmony, powerfully influence the mind and are therefore one of the bases of civilization. Fletcher of Saltoun expressed the Greek view when he said that "if a man were permitted to make all the ballads, he need not care who should make the laws of a nation."

Already in the 19th century, Nietzsche detected in Europe a "brutalization and decay of rhythm." Generalizations are over-simple, but the culture that has to a great extent replaced the old poetic culture values cacophony rather than harmony, brokenness rather than wholeness, and ungraceful forms of order rather than those grounded in poetic rhythm. The new culture—a significant force in education, popular entertainment and the arts, and modern architecture and town planning—has much less unifying power than the old culture; its perfection lies not in the organic whole but in the isolated fragment. Eliot, indeed, formed *The Waste Land* out of poetic fragments in part because he was attempting to render, in verse, the effect on the mind of the desolate and fragmented waste land he found modern life to be.

Whatever its merits, the new culture has failed to give people the tools they need to amalgamate disparate experience and perceive what the Greeks called the "wholeness of life." Dissatisfied and profoundly isolated, confined, in Tocqueville's image, "within the solitude of his own heart," the modern man, and in particular the modern man who comes from the well-to-do and predominantly agnostic classes, seeks consolation in the various and always inadequate intellectual and spiritual opiums on sale in the philosophical markets—Marxism, psychoanalysis, multiculturalism, Weatherman-style radicalism, the pharmaceutical eucharist of the anti-depressant tablet.

Obama is, if not quite the messiah of this new culture, certainly an artifact of it. He discovered early that what he calls his "story," that of a multi-racial prophet equally at home at Harvard and in the slums, struck the profoundest chords in desolate upper-caste hearts. Middle America, by contrast, has mixed feelings about the new culture. It has embraced television and adjusted to a new set of musical rhythms, but it remains suspicious of other elements of the modernist and progressive sensibility. Obama's healer-redeemer qualities, which find so warm a reception in the hearts of the elites, make Joe Six-Pack uneasy. Were it not for the coincidence of his candidacy with a stock-market panic, the Democratic nominee's campaign for the White House would almost certainly end in failure. But the stock market crashed, and as a result Obama is, at this writing, the front-runner.

The conservative case against Obama goes beyond both questions of policy and questions about his record and background. Obama is widely regarded, by his supporters, as a visionary statesman, yet nowhere in his rhetoric does he bring this visionary power to bear on the most pressing problem of the age, the vulnerability of the old culture of the West, which is the ultimate source of its freedoms.

The omission is disconcerting. Like Obama, I am a graduate of Columbia College. I arrived on the campus in the fall of 1984, a little more than a year after he took his degree. I understand that he almost never speaks of Columbia, and to do him justice, there was much that was grim in pre-Giuliani Morningside Heights. But Columbia nevertheless had (and still has) its Core Curriculum, a group of obligatory courses in literature, art, and music that force the student to come to terms with the miracle of Western civilization—with the Greeks, Virgil, Dante, and Shakespeare; with Montaigne, Locke, Hume, Smith, Marx, and Mill; with Bach and Beethoven and Mozart. Of course you don't take it all in at 18 or 19, but even so the Core is bound to be one of the memorable intellectual experiences of a thoughtful person's life.

Yet the Core seems to have made little impression on Barack Obama. Its themes find no echo in his reflection on politics, *The Audacity of Hope*. Thucydides, describing the plague at Athens, showed that the virtues which characterize Western civilization at its best—freedom, a sense of fair play, a consciousness of the dignity of human life—cannot be taken for granted. Obama is much less attentive to the fragility of the West's peculiar culture. In Berlin he spoke of tearing down the walls that separate Western nations from the rest of the world: "People of the world—this is our moment. This is our time. . . . There is no challenge too great for a world that stands as one. . . . The walls between the countries with the most and those with the least cannot stand." This wall-wrecking sentiment is in some ways admirable, but those with a heritage as unique as ours can consent to such a demolition only if we are certain that the culture that has made us what we are will afterwards be safe.

When Obama *does* speak of the value of American culture and the larger civilization of which it is a part, there is invariably a false note. As "long as I live," he said in Philadelphia in March, "I will never forget that in no other country on earth is my story even possible." The worthiness of the conviction is tempered by its narcissism; it is as though Pericles, in his funeral oration, offered as proof of the greatness of Athens the fact that it had made his own "story" possible.

Barack Obama is not the right leader to preside over this moment of crisis in the West, when the old civilization is dying in Europe and has lost its hold on the greater part of this country's ruling classes. John McCain is the better choice: His experience has given him a keener sense of history and of the world. Some people are skilled in talking about the defense of freedom and civilization; McCain has actually defended them. He is not so stirring an orator as the senator from Illinois. But he has only to walk into the room, and his presence sounds the theme.

January 25, 2010

A Most Uncomfortable Parallel

What Clement Attlee can teach the Right about Barack Obama

By Andrew Stuttaford

L et's just agree that if you are looking for someone with whom to compare Barack Obama, the mid-20th-century British prime minister Clement Attlee does not come *immediately* to mind. Some might opt for FDR, some the Messiah, others the Antichrist or, harsher still, Jimmy Carter. Attlee? Not so much.

To start with, there's the whole charisma thing. Attlee was the Labour leader who humiliated Winston Churchill in Britain's 1945 election, but that victory (one of the most sweeping in British history) was more dramatic than the victor. No Obama, the new prime minister was shy, understated, and physically unprepossessing. Balding, sober-suited, and with an unshakeable aura of bourgeois respectability, Attlee resembled a senior bureaucrat, a provincial bank manager, or one of the more upscale varieties of traditional English murderer. If you want an adjective, "dull" will do nicely. As the jibe went, an empty taxi drew up, and out stepped Attlee. His speeches were dreary, largely unmemorable, and marked mainly by a reluctance to deploy the personal pronoun: Not for Attlee the "I"s and "me"s of Obama's perorations. Clem was a modest man, but then, said some, he had much to be modest about.

That's an insult that's often attributed to Winston Churchill, but almost certainly incorrectly: Churchill had considerable respect for the individual who defeated him. Realize why and comparisons between the stiff, taciturn Englishman and America's president begin to make sense. For the GOP, they are good reason to be alarmed.

There are the superficial similarities, of both character and résumé. Despite their very distinct camouflages both men are best understood as being cool and calculating, not least in their use of an unthreatening public persona to mask the intensity of their beliefs and ambitions. The two even have in common their pasts as "community organizers," in Attlee's case as a charity worker amid the poverty of Edwardian London's East End, a harrowing and intoxicating experience that drove him to socialism. More important still is their shared eye for the main chance. In a private 1936 memo, Attlee (by then leader of his party) noted how any future European war would involve "the closest regimentation of the whole nation" and as such "the opportunity for fundamental change of the economic system." Never let a crisis go to waste.

Attlee was right. In 1940 the Labour party was asked to join Churchill's new national coalition government (with Attlee serving as deputy prime minister), and it wasn't long before Britain had been reengineered into what was for all practical purposes a command economy. The extension of the state's grasp was theoretically temporary and realistically unavoidable, but it quickly became obvious that the assault on laissez faire would outlive the wartime emergency. The crisis had overturned the balance of power between the public and private sectors. It was a shift that, when combined with Britons' widespread perception of pre-war economic, military, and diplomatic failure, also shattered the longstanding political taboos that would once have ensured a return to business as usual when the conflict came to an end. With Britain's *ancien régime* discredited (it's debatable quite how fairly), there was irresistible demand for "change." Prevailing over the Axis would, most Britons hoped, mean that they could finally turn the page on the bad old days and build the fairer, more egalitarian society they felt they deserved.

It is a measure of how far the political landscape had been altered that by March 1943 Winston Churchill was announcing his support for the establishment after the war of "a National Health Service . . . [and] national compulsory insurance for all classes for all purposes from the cradle to the grave," a stance that echoed an official report published to extraordinary acclaim the previous year. Churchill did, however, take time to warn that it would be necessary to take account of what the country could afford before these schemes were implemented.

Such concerns were alien to Attlee. The abrupt end of American aid in the form of the Lend-Lease program within a month of the Labour victory had left the U.K. facing, in Keynes's words, a "financial Dunkirk." The clouds cleared a little with the grant of a large, if tough-termed, U.S. loan, but the risk of national bankruptcy remained real for some years. Attlee pressed on regardless. The creation of the welfare state was his overwhelming moral and political priority. He had been presented with a possibly unrepeatable opportunity to push it through, and that's what he did. To carp was mere bean counting. If there were any gaps, they could surely be filled by the improvements that would come from the government's supposedly superior management of the economy and, of course, by hiking taxes on "the rich" still further. Is this unpleasantly reminiscent of the manner in which Obama has persisted with his broader agenda in the face of the greatest economic crunch in over half a century? Oh yes.

There's also more than a touch of Obama in the way that Attlee viewed foreign policy and defense. A transnationalist *avant la lettre*, the prime minister thought that empowering the United Nations at the expense of its members was the only true guarantor of national security, a position that made his inability or unwillingness to grasp the meaning of either "national" or "security" embarrassingly clear. It is no surprise that he was reluctant to accept the inevitability of the Cold War with a Soviet Union already on the rampage. Attlee would, I reckon, have sympathized with Obama's hesitations in the face of today's Islamic challenge. Mercifully, reality—and the U.K.'s tough-minded foreign secretary—soon intervened. Britain adopted a more robust approach to its national defense (sometimes misguidedly; too many resources were devoted to an unsustainable commitment to some of the more worthless scraps of empire) and a place in the front line against Soviet expansion. In a sense, however, Attlee was to have the last laugh; the long-term damage that his government inflicted on the British economy meant that, even apart from the huge costs of the country's post-war imperial over-stretch, its decline to lesser-power status was inevitable.

But judged on his own terms, Attlee succeeded where it counted most. His nationalization of a key slice of British industry (including the railways, some road transport, gas, coal, iron and steel, the Bank of England, and even Thomas Cook, the travel agency) eventually proved disastrous; his intrusive regulatory and planning regime (not to speak of the crippling taxes he promoted) distorted the economy and retarded development for decades; the costs of the new National Health Service (NHS) instantly spiraled beyond what had been anticipated; and so on and on and on—but, well, never mind. In the greater scheme of things, he won. To this ascetic, high-minded statesman, GDP was a grubby detail and budgets were trivia. What mattered was that he had irrevocably committed Britain to the welfare state he believed to be an ethical imperative—and the NHS was its centerpiece.

And yes, that commitment *was* irrevocable. While a majority of Britons approved of including health care in their wish list for the postwar renewal of their nation, socialized medicine had not been amongst their top priorities. But once set up (in 1948), the NHS proved immediately and immensely popular, a "right" untouchable by any politician. For all the grumbling, it still is. The electoral dynamics of the NHS (which directly employs well over a million voters) were and are different from those of the likely Obamacare, not least because the private system the NHS replaced was far feebler than that, however flawed, which now operates in the U.S. Nevertheless, the lessons to be drawn from the story of the NHS form part of a picture that is bad news for those who hope that GOP wins in 2010 will shatter Barack's dream.

At first sight, the fact that Attlee barely scraped reelection five years after his 1945 triumph would seem to suggest the opposite, but to secure any majority in the wake of half a decade of savage economic retrenchment was a remarkable achievement. The transformation of which the NHS represented such a vital part (and the events that made that transformation possible) had radically shifted the terms of debate within the U.K. to the left and, no less crucially, reinforced Labour's political base. To remain electorally competitive, the Tories (who finally unseated Attlee the following year) were forced to accept the essence of Labour's remodeling of the British state, something they broadly continued to do until the arrival of Mrs. Thatcher as Conservative leader a generation later. It's no great stretch to suspect that a GOP chastened by the Bush years and intimidated by the obstacles that lie ahead will be just as cautious in tackling the Obama legacy.

And that *will* be something to be modest about.

July 5, 2010

The Obama Enigma

Disconnection from the main currents of American life turns out to be a political disadvantage

By Ramesh Ponnuru

'I serve as a blank screen on which people of vastly different political stripes project their own views," Barack Obama famously wrote in the prologue to *The Audacity of Hope*. He wrote as though this "blankness" were not part of a conscious strategy for winning the White House. It was the emptiness of his slogans—"we are the ones we've been waiting for"—that allowed liberals and moderates to consider him a soul mate. Being enigmatic also enabled him to be glamorous. Coolness and distance are not just an Obama strategy; they are also clearly integral to his personality. But they are a strategy.

That strategy has a flipside, which is that his opponents can project unattractive qualities on them. And oh have they tried. At the outer edges of our politics (and sanity) are those who affix to Obama an identity as a Muslim, or an Indonesian. At the beginning of his presidency, mainstream Republicans were wary of attacking the president personally. But that reticence lasted only a few weeks. Since then they have ventured to define him in several ways, all negative. He is weak and indecisive, they have said, especially during the drawn-out debate over his Afghanistan policy. He was acting like an "Ivy League professor," holding "seminars" instead of acting. At other times his opponents have said he is a machine politician: a practitioner of "the Chicago way." He is a radical. An elitist. A liar—as Rep. Joe Wilson shouted.

During the 2008 campaign, Karl Rove described him as someone who coasts on his charm rather than doing hard work. A Republican Web ad, similarly, portrayed him as a "celebrity." Since he got elected, Republicans have labeled him "whiny" whenever he has blamed the

182

nation's, or his own, troubles on the Bush administration, and "petulant" whenever he has attacked current Republicans. "Vain" and "arrogant" are also words they have attached to him.

Obama's sharpest mainstream critics have questioned his patriotism. When it comes to "identification with the nation and to all that binds its people together in pride and allegiance," *Wall Street Journal* columnist Dorothy Rabinowitz recently wrote, the president is deficient. "He is the alien in the White House." As oil has kept spilling into the Gulf of Mexico, even some of the president's fans have taken to faulting him for showing too much aloofness and not enough emotion. They too believe that he is detached, even if they will not add "from his countrymen."

Not all of these critiques make sense, or hang together very well. Republicans might try to portray Obama as weak and indecisive toward the country's enemies and savage with his domestic opponents; but they are not going to convince the public that Obama the man is simultaneously ruthless and weak. A kind of elitism may well be inherent in his political philosophy, but the imputation of snobbery to our first black president, who was raised without a father, is inapt.

On the other hand, some of the charges stick. Obama is in some respects more liberal than previous Democratic presidents, and the evidence his defenders use to deny this fact consists chiefly of tactical retreats. Not fighting for single payer or a public option when Congress would not have passed either proves that he can count votes, not that he is a moderate. He is vain, even as successful politicians go: How many other politicians would say that they are better strategists than their strategist, better speechwriters than their speechwriter, etc.? He is thin-skinned: Has he ever responded to a criticism with self-deprecating humor, or grace? He regularly has an unpresidential air of being put upon. "Lying" is a strong term, but Obama also frequently says things that one would think he knows not to be true—such as that people who like their current health plans will be able to keep them under his reform.

Some of the critiques have clearly gotten to Obama. He told Matt Lauer that he spoke to experts about the oil spill so he would "know whose ass to kick." He was defending himself against the charge of being academic, unemotional, and passive. It was not, perhaps, the most persuasive thing this president has ever said. (At least he did not promise to create a new Department of Kick-Assery to be staffed by the best and brightest.)

The president was, of course, overcompensating. But he was also condescending. Perhaps all of the encomia to him for being uncommonly thoughtful have gone to his head. He assumes that the public will see the point of reason only if it is translated into terms of brute force.

Obama has long been considered an exceptionally talented politician, but he lacks some of the basic political skills one expects of the breed. He does not have an instinctive feel for the country's mood, and so he cannot find the right pitch—even, or especially, at moments of high national anxiety. President Clinton's reaction to the Oklahoma City bombing revived his presidency. This president, following the shootings at Fort Hood, proved incapable of rallying the country. His initial remarks were off-key, coming as they did after praise to some of his staffers and a "shout-out" to a distinguished member of the audience at a previously planned Tribal Nations Conference. Obama then allowed top officials to suggest that sacrificing "diversity" would be a greater tragedy than the massacre.

It can be said in Obama's defense that at a far more crucial moment, his predecessor delivered a more dismaying performance. President Bush's remarks on the evening of September 11 were the opposite of reassuring. But Bush righted himself within days at Ground Zero. It is hard to imagine this president grabbing the bullhorn.

In part Obama's deficiency is a function of the inexperience that his opponents warned against during the 2008 campaign. Obama pledged to close Guantanamo Bay within a year of his inauguration. A more experienced leader might not have had any illusions about the progress from wish to reality. With more time on Capitol Hill, he might also have seen the dangers of letting the Democratic caucus set the legislative agenda. The president could have gotten a bipartisan stimulus if he had cut in big-spending Republicans—and who can doubt he would be in better shape now if he had?

But the deeper problem is Obama's disconnection from the major currents of American life. The country has been a commercial republic since its beginning; Obama has had almost no contact with business life.

He also grew up in a much more left-wing milieu than any of his prede-cessors, and than the vast majority of Americans. During the campaign, he remarked that he was glad to be in Henry Wallace's home county. How many people his age think fondly of Wallace? (Reported *Politico*: "'I was amazed that he knew about Henry Wallace,' said Diane Weiland, the longtime director of the Henry A. Wallace Country Life Center, who was in the audience.")

Americans knew Barack Obama was to the left of most Americans when they elected him. They do not believe that he is a socialist. They do not think—at least yet—that he is untrustworthy. But some charges against leaders have a long fuse. Liberal charges that President Bush was a liar and a fool did not persuade Americans during his first term, but helped to poison his second. Americans may start to think that Obama is arrogant, and that he does not understand them. Those perceptions will be devastating if they also conclude that he's not up to the job.